ROSE GARDENS

ROSE GARDENS

—Their History and Design—

JANE FEARNLEY-WHITTINGSTALL

HENRY HOLT AND COMPANY
NEW YORK

for J.H.C.L.

Published in the United States by
Henry Holt and Company, Inc., 115 West 18th Street,
New York, New York 10011.
Published in Canada by Fitzhenry & Whiteside Limited,
195 Allstate Parkway, Markham, Ontario L3R 4T8.

Library of Congress Catalog Card Number: 89–45381

ISBN 0–8050–1144–7

Henry Holt books are available at special discounts for bulk
purchases for sales promotions, premiums, fund-raising, or
educational use. Special editions or book excerpts can also be
created to specification.

For details contact:

Special Sales Director
Henry Holt and Company, Inc.
115 West 18th Street
New York, New York 10011

First American Edition

Designed by Chatto & Windus Ltd., London
Printed in Great Britain
10 9 8 7 6 5 4 3 2 1

Half title page 'Bouquet des Fleurs' from *Les Roses*, vol. I, by
Pierre-Joseph Redouté, 1817.

Frontispiece In the gardens at Castle Howard.

Part titles From John Gerard's *Herbal*, 1597.

Contents

Preface

It seems right to make some sort of apology, as most of my predecessors have done, for putting forth another Rose-book when there are already so many.

Revd A. Foster-Melliar *The Book of the Rose*

If Foster-Melliar felt the need for such an apology in 1894, what excuse can I possibly have, close to a century later, and many, many rose books later, for attempting to add to the literature of the rose?

My justification is that, whilst there is no shortage of excellent guides to the cultivation of the rose, numerous alluring picture books of roses of all kinds and informative, generously illustrated catalogues from leading rose nurseries, the subject of the rose garden, as opposed to the rose, has been neglected.

I have set out to trace the history of rose gardens, to analyse those that succeed as gardens in their own right, rather than as collections of roses, to examine the materials available today for making rose gardens, and to describe examples of rose gardens that I have found beautiful and inspiring. I have seen more of the latter than I would have imagined possible before I started my search and I am grateful to the many kind owners who allowed me to visit their gardens and who shared with me their knowledge and delight in roses and their skill in using roses to create gardens that are so much more than the sum of their parts. It is sad that a finite number of pages allows me to describe only a few and readers may wonder how I could be so insensitive as to omit their favourite. In making my selection, I have tried to show gardens of varied sizes and styles which will, I hope, offer ideas that can be adapted for a variety of sites.

It is because of the generosity of the owners of gardens large and small, formal and informal, on chalk, clay and sand, in sheltered enclosures and on windswept hillsides, that I can now invite you, in the words of the distinguished rosarian clergyman Dean Hole, to 'enter the Rose-garden when the first sunshine sparkles in the dew, and enjoy with thankful happiness one of the loveliest scenes of earth'.

Climbing roses on an iron pergola at Roseraie de l'Haÿ near Paris.

Introduction

Why roses? How has it come about that the rose is to be found not only in gardens throughout the world but in paintings and poetry, in myths and legends, as the badge of dynasties and the emblem of nations as far from each other geographically and culturally as Czechoslovakia, England, Honduras, Iran, Poland and Romania? The rose has also entered daily life as no other flower has: I have never sought out the rose as a decorative motif, but when I look around me I find that, when I get up in the morning, I open curtains covered in chintz roses and drink my breakfast coffee from a rose-decorated mug. I can bath in rose-scented water using rose-scented soap which sits in a dish with a border of rosebuds. If I go to church on Sunday I will find the stone-flagged floor lit by fragments of coloured light filtered through a rose window and I can use a rosary as an aid to prayer. If my mind wanders I can contemplate the silk rose in the hat of the woman in the pew in front of me. Church can be followed by a pre-lunch drink at the Rose and Crown. This may bring the roses to my cheeks and cause me to see the world through rose-coloured spectacles. But I must beware of flaunting a red rose in my buttonhole lest it be taken as an indication of my political sympathies. Even outside the garden, the rose is everywhere.

As for gardens, there is hardly a plot in Britain, from the grandest to the tiniest, without at least one rose bush, and the same is true of most gardens in Europe. Roses have even given their name to other flowers so that, besides 'real' roses, I can find in my own garden, at different seasons, a Christmas rose, a lenten rose, a primrose, rosemary, rose of Sharon, rose acacia, rose geranium, rose-campion, a sun rose and a rock rose. Everything in the garden is rosy.

Today it does not seem surprising that the rose has become supreme among flowers in our imagery as well as in our gardens: its ubiquity and versatility almost guarantee it. No other flower is found in such a variety of shapes, sizes and colours, ranging from the innocent freshness of *R. hugonis* with its single, prim-rose-coloured flowers to the dusky opulence of 'Cardinal de Richelieu' or the neon gaudiness of 'Super Star'. No other shrub

The very free-flowering *Rosa complicata* with a contrasting spire of *Digitalis purpurea*.

3

can fulfil such a variety of roles. Miniature Polyantha roses decorate window boxes with demure charm. Dense, near-ever-green Wichuraianas suppress weeds over large areas. *R. filipes* and its relations sprawl and cascade from the tops of mature beech trees. Floribunda roses neatly fill parterre beds with solid masses of colour, and the brave and hardy Rugosas resist pollution to brighten the central reservations of motorways.

Yet it is only comparatively recently that such a wealth of roses has been available to inspire gardeners, poets, painters, writers and designers. Before the journeys of the great plant hunters brought rose species to Europe from other continents and before the revolution in hybridisation at the start of the nineteenth century, the only roses available were species native to a particular area and their accidental sports and hybrids.

Nevertheless, early in the history of civilisation the rose was found to be both beautiful and useful. It was brought into the first gardens for its supposed medicinal properties, for the value of its scent and for the beauty of its flowers in garlands to decorate priests and sacrificial victims. It captured the imagination of poets and myth-makers, partly, perhaps, because of the paradox presented by the power of a thing of such guileless beauty to wound with its thorns.

When planning a rose garden, or deciding where to place a rose bush among other plants, we think in terms of soil and aspect, of colour schemes and scents, of planting distances, of the relative heights of plants, and of the foliage and shapes of companion plants. But, great as is the satisfaction to be gained from getting all these things right (and heaven knows it is hard enough), there is an additional dimension to the pleasure of a rose garden which is not often considered: it is the enjoyment of knowing something of the history of the rose, and its role in our literature and art. Who, if they wanted to grow roses at all, could not wish to include some old roses for their associations as well as for their beauty and scent? The Holy Rose of Abyssinia, the White Rose of York and the Red Rose of Lancaster, the rose from Omar Khayyam's tomb, 'in a spot where the North Wind may scatter Roses over it' are irresistibly romantic. My own delight in the beauty of the Alba rose 'Celestial' is enhanced by knowing that it was Henry VIII's favourite among the roses at Hampton Court, and when I contemplate 'Marie Louise' with her full, rich pink,

Pink and white roses set off by the pale yellows of *Alchemilla mollis*, herbaceous potentillas and santolina at Heale House, Wiltshire.

Heale House, Wiltshire.

strongly scented blooms, it pleases me to know that she was bred for the Empress Josephine at Malmaison by the same M. Eugène Hardy who named the most beautiful of all white roses after his wife.

Such thoughts help to make a rose garden a place of contemplation, a place which can approach the Persian ideal of a Paradise 'where man composes his soul and is at one with his world'.

PART ONE

❦

The History of Roses in the Garden

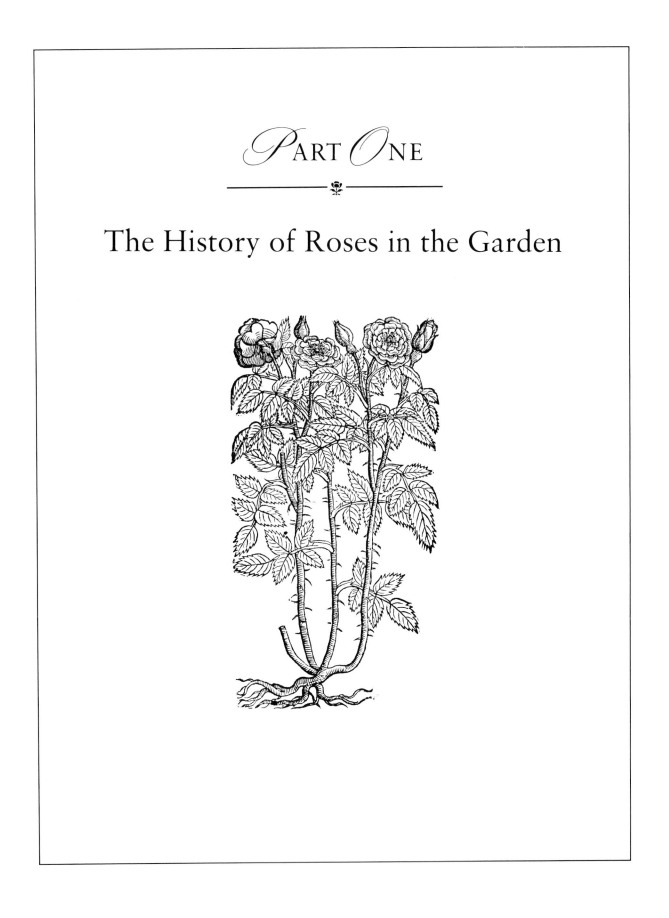

CHAPTER ONE

Early Rose Gardens

Anacreon and Bion sang the rose;
And Rhodes the isle whose very name means rose
Struck roses on her coins;
Pliny made lists and Roman libertines
Made wreaths to wear among the flutes and wines;
The young crusaders found the Syrian rose
Springing from Saracenic quoins,
And China opened her shut gate
To let her roses through, the Persian shrines
Of poetry and painting gave the rose.

Vita Sackville-West *The Garden*

There were wild roses in the world before there was man: their existence at least thirty-two million years ago is indicated by fossils discovered in Colorado and Oregon. It is also certain that, from pre-historic times, rose species were growing, and still are, throughout the northern hemisphere.

We have to leap forward to about 3000 BC to find a connection between man and the rose, to Ancient Egypt where the rose was sacred to the goddess Isis, and where traces of what may be *R. richardii*, also known as the Holy Rose of Abyssinia, have been found in tombs. The finely wrought golden image of a horned ram caught in a rose thicket, excavated at Sumer, was made at about the same time, and excavations at Ur and Akkad found evidence that, between 2845 and 2768 BC, Sargon, the king of Sumer and Akkad, crossed the River Taurus on a military expedition and brought back 'vines, fig trees and rose trees' to the Tigris–Euphrates delta.

We have to wait for the Greeks for any firm evidence of aesthetic appreciation of the rose. The Greeks were not great gardeners, perhaps because the landscapes they inhabited, although of great natural beauty and grandeur, were not easy to cultivate. It therefore seems likely that Homer's image of 'rosy-fingered dawn' and the representations of roses that he described on the shield of Achilles and the helmet of Hector (the impartial rose favouring both the Greeks and the Trojans) were based on his appreciation

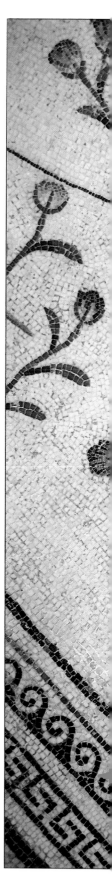

'Spring'. Detail of the Neptune mosaic from Chebra, Tunisia, 2nd century AD.

of roses growing in the wild rather than cultivated forms.

About a century on from Homer, in the fifth century B C, Herodotus describes the Gardens of Midas in Phrygia as having roses 'so sweet that no others can vie with them and their blossoms have as many as sixty petals'. A hundred years later, golden earrings from Thrace are decorated with rosettes based on both single and semi-double roses, but they do not show the fullness of Herodotus' sixty petals. By 300 B C, however, Theophrastus in his *Enquiry into Plants* was able to describe roses as having any number of petals from five to one hundred. At this time too, the coins mentioned in Vita Sackville-West's poem were being struck in Rhodes where roses were used in the worship of Aphrodite, and the Egyptians were depicting roses on textiles and in frescos and using them in funeral garlands.

The Romans were practical about agriculture and horticulture but they also enjoyed flowers for their own sake. The first Latin Primer I learned from began with *puella in horto*, which has made me think of the Romans as keen gardeners ever since I first struggled with the ablative case. In Rome flowers, including roses, were cultivated both commercially and in private gardens. Virgil, in the *Georgics* Book I V, mentions beds at Paestum of double-flowering roses, and the festival of Rosalia on the island of Samos was held twice a year, in May and again in September, indicating that the repeat-flowering Damask roses must have been in cultivation, giving greater scope for gardeners than ever before.

Virgil also described the garden of an old man of Corcyrus. His land was too poor for grazing or even for vines, but he managed to make a garden. It was bordered with white lilies, verbena and poppies, and contained hyacinths and roses and numerous trees planted in rows. It sounds very pretty. Horace, however, far from extolling roses, disapproved of the conversion of cornfields into rose fields. Probably such a rose farm was the nearest thing to a rose garden for most of the Romans. The fields of roses grown as a cash crop must have looked very much the same as those which supply scent factories today, in Bulgaria and at Grasse in the south of France, making bold blocks of pink among the grey-green olive groves of the Mediterranean landscape.

The Romans of the Empire put the rose crop to many and varied uses. The legendary decadence of the later emperors, their courtiers and their courtesans, and their eagerness to – in Swinburne's lines –

> *Change in a trice*
> *The lilies and langours of virtue*
> *For the raptures and roses of vice.*

fed the families of farmers in the Campagna as well as feeding the fancies of subsequent poets and artists. Cicero, old spoilsport that he was, deplored the practice of eating one's dinner reclining on rose petals. What censorious eloquence he might have used to condemn Nero's expenditure (as reported by Suetonius) of four million sesterces on roses for one feast. The excesses of Nero and succeeding emperors, particularly Heliogabalus, who was brought up in the fleshpots of Syria and therefore surprised nobody by his effeminate and luxury-loving way of life, included rose-water flowing from fountains indoors and out, rose-scented wine, cushions stuffed with rose-petals, floors covered in them, and rose-water as hang-over cure and love potion.

That sort of thing could give roses a bad name, so it is with relief that we can turn to Pliny the Younger who gave a detailed description of a pleasure garden featuring roses. He was a talented garden designer, a lover of roses and a man of letters. It was his uncle, Pliny the Elder, who suggested that Britain must have been named Albion because of the profusion of white roses that grew there. If it is a fiction, it is the kind of fiction that is more appealing than fact. He also listed twelve varieties of rose and wrote in some detail about its medicinal properties, giving a concoction of honey, rose vinegar, rose water and dried seed as a cure for sore throats, ulcerated gums, headaches, earaches, piles, nausea, stomach-ache, toothache, fluxes of the eyebrows, diarrhoea, haemorrhage, eye trouble, hypochondria and mange. Pliny also recommended burnt petals as a cosmetic for the eyebrows and powdered petals as a deodorant. It is not surprising that Strabo could write some 700 years later, 'No man can say, no man remember, how many uses there are for Oil of Roses as a cure for Mankind's ailments.'

After the fall of the western Roman Empire in 476 there is a gap in our knowledge of the history of the rose as an ornamental plant, but its cultivation certainly continued for the sake of its perfume and its medicinal properties.

CHAPTER TWO

Cloister and Court

Among all floures of the world the floure of the rose is chief and beeryth ye pryse ... For by fayrness they feed the syghte, and playseth the smell by odour, the touch by soft handlynge. And wythstondeth and socouryth by vertue against many syknesses and evrylles.

Bartholomeus Anglicus, *De Proprietatibus Rerum* (1398)

In the so-called Dark Ages, the Christian church became the centre of learning and monastic manuscripts the source of information about medicine and horticulture. Such writings deal mainly with vegetables and herbs; few flowers are mentioned apart from those with culinary or medicinal uses, but when flowers are listed at all, roses and lilies are nearly always included. Alcuin of York grew lilies and roses outside his monastic cell at Tours in the eighth century and Walafrid Strabo, writing around 840 on the monastic garden at Reichenau, calls the rose 'the flower of flowers'. For him the red rose symbolised blood shed by the blessed martyrs and the lily was 'a shining sign of the faith'.

From this time onwards, knowledge about plants and seeds and cuttings of new varieties spread gradually through Europe with the monks of the Benedictine Order. In about 1092 King William Rufus visited the garden of the Benedictine nuns at Romsey Abbey; his excuse was 'to look at the roses and other flowering herbs', but it is said that he was also keen to take a look at the lovely young Lady Eadgyth who was an inmate of the convent. But it would be a mistake to suppose that no gardening went on outside the cloistered security of religious houses. As early as the third century AD there is a description by Longus in *Daphnis and Chloë* of the garden of Lamon. Although this is a fictional, fantasy garden, it must bear some relation to real gardens that the poet knew. He described it as 'a thing of beauty ... fit for a prince.' Fruit trees and vines grew inside a boundary of cypress, laurel, pine and plane trees 'like a palisade built by hand'. There were 'beds of various flowers, some the earth's own sowing, some that man had sown. The roses, hyacinths, and lilies were cultivated by hand; the violets, narcissus and pimpernel were the earth's gift.'

Above An illustration from Gerard's *Herbal* (1597).

Right A medieval Paradise Garden with flowery meadow and rose arbour: *La Vierge à la Roseraie* by Stefano da Verona (early 15th century).

Such pleasure gardens would certainly have been the preserve of kings and princes in fact as well as fiction. In France, in 550 AD, King Childebert arranged for a rose garden to be planted for his wife, Ultregote, and much later Charlemagne included roses and lilies among the plants for his model garden. Later still, in 1275, King Edward I's garden at the Tower of London contained several hundred red and white roses.

It is a matter for speculation to what extent flowering plants, including roses, were appreciated and cultivated for their beauty rather than their usefulness. After the fall of the Roman Empire, many centuries were to pass before garden design would again reach the sophistication of Pliny's villa gardens, but the art of gardening never completely died out, whilst the craft of horticulture continued to flourish. The Benedictine monks were not the only travellers to export plants from city to city and from country to country. New roses were probably being brought into Europe from the seventh century onwards by Islamic conquerors. Coming from their conquest of Persia, where roses had long been appreciated and cultivated, they introduced roses to Spain and thence to the rest of Europe, and later, in the tenth century, eastwards to India. From the time when the Moors came to Spain and throughout the period of the Crusades there would have been a cross-fertilisation of ideas about gardens. The Apothecary's Rose (*R. gallica* 'Officinalis') is thought to have been brought to Europe during the crusades by Thibaut VI; it became the heraldic device of the Lancastrians when Eleanor of Aquitaine brought it to England at the time of her marriage to Henry II.

Henry II's name is connected with another rose with a romantic tradition: *Rosa gallica* 'Versicolor', or 'Rosa Mundi', is associated with his mistress, Fair Rosamund, and is also thought to have been brought back from the Crusades. A striped rose must have been something very special in the twelfth century and tradition has it that Rosamund Clifford was very special too. The king installed her in a 'House of Daedalus', presumably surrounded by a labyrinth or maze, in his park at Woodstock, which also became known as 'Rosamund's Bower'. Perhaps she planted 'Rosa Mundi' around it. Rosamund died young, reputedly poisoned by the jealous queen. Her tomb bears an epitaph made up of untranslatable Latin puns:

Woodcuts illustrating the *Roman de la Rose* (c. 1481) show primitive gardens enclosed by wattle fences.

Hic jacet in tumba
Rosa mundi, non rosa munda;
Non redolet, sed olet,
Quae redolere solet.

The gist of it is that, like the girl in the song, Rosamund was very much a 'second-hand Rose', and the scent emanating from her grave was certainly not that of roses.

Long before the rose was widely appreciated in Europe, it was supreme in the gardens of Persia and we owe much to the Arabs who invaded Persia in the seventh century AD, to their quick assimilation of Persian arts, including the art of gardening, and to their fervent campaign to carry the Islamic religion all over the known world. Persian gardens were invariably laid out in the same pattern of four areas divided by paths or water channels in the shape of a cross. This layout symbolised the four quarters of the universe divided by four great rivers. The cruciform pattern of these gardens, their private, enclosed nature, the use of water and of shade-giving trees for refreshment in desert climates, and the appreciation that the Persians felt for the beauty of flowers were all well adapted to fit the sensual descriptions of Paradise in the Koran, and in due course gardens were created which aspired to resemble Paradise throughout the Moslem world, from Spain to India.

The rose was of great significance in Islamic culture. It is said to have sprung from drops of the Prophet's sweat which fell to the earth during his journey to Paradise, and the image of the rose and of rose gardens is used again and again by philosophers and poets. Omar Khayyam, the Persian poet, scholar and mathematician who died in 1123, and whose *Rubaiyat* is widely known and loved thanks to Edward Fitzgerald's translation, filled his poetry with the imagery of roses and wished to be buried where rose petals would blow on to his grave. His wish was granted by posterity. Many centuries later, in 1884, hips collected from the roses on his tomb were brought to Kew in England and roses raised from them were planted on Fitzgerald's grave as well.

The rose seems to have retained its power in Islamic culture to fuse the mystic with the sensual, and to have maintained its dominance in gardens wherever the Persian influence has penetrated. In 1593, 50,000 white roses were ordered for the

Palace at Topkapisaray in Turkey. In India, the English traveller
Peter Mundy, visiting Akbar's tomb at Sikandra in 1632,
described the gardens as planted with roses in abundance. The
gardens of Babur at Agra and Jehangir in Kashmir and at Shah
Dara were also famous for their roses. In Persia the eleventh
century garden of Bagh-i-Takht was visited in 1678 by Tavernier
who mentions fruit trees and rose trees in plenty.

It is a delightfully romantic notion that roses were discovered
springing from 'Saracenic quoins' in the Holy Land by crusading
knights and brought home to grace the gardens of France, Flanders
and England, but there is no firm evidence to support the theory.
I like to imagine that flower of chivalry, the 'parfit gentle knight',
making his way home after winning his battle for Christendom
with his precious rose bush in his baggage, keeping it alive and
safe through all the vicissitudes of thirteenth-century travel in
order to present it as a token of love at his journey's end. Perhaps
he would then wish to recreate at home the kind of garden where
the rose had first charmed him, and to set out in a courtyard of
his castle the simple, symmetrical pattern of an Islamic Paradise
garden. But it is just as likely that both the roses and the garden
style of Islam were discovered for Europe nearer to home, when

Above left Detail of a painting
on the fountain in the bedroom
of Murad, Topkapi Palace,
Istanbul.

Above right Mehmed II by
Sinan Bey, 16th century,
Topkapi Palace.

Right Roman de la Rose. The
Lover attains the Rose. Flemish,
c. 1500.

16

La conclusion du roimmant

Christians recaptured the Islamic city of Cordoba in Spain in 1034, after 300 years of Arab rule.

Thereafter monastic writers and artists took possession of the rose's symbolic role and gradually it became known as the Virgin Mary's flower. Gardens connected with monasteries, planted with roses and furnished with fountains, walks and arbours, were known as 'Mary Gardens'. These would probably have been laid out in the same form as an Islamic Paradise garden, but with a very different symbolic purpose. They, too, would have been in the shape of a cross, with paths dividing the space into four. Thus the garden of the True Believer came to resemble that of the 'Infidel'.

In the twelfth century secular gardens, too, were becoming more ornamental. Alexander Neckham wrote in *De Naturibus Rerum,* 'The Garden should be adorned with roses and lilies, turnsok [heliotrope], violets and mandrake.' Most of his book was concerned with 'useful' plants, vegetables and herbs, but his use of the word 'adorn' seems to indicate that the aesthetic as well as the practical value of gardening had become important. At about the same time, *La Roman de la Rose* appeared in France. Guillaume de Lorris' popular allegorical poem was produced in several versions and the manuscripts include illustrations of gardens with roses prominent among the flowers. They are among the earliest pictorial records of gardens.

The practical aspects of making a garden are dealt with by Petrus de Crescentiis, writing in Italy in 1305. He recommends enclosing it with ditches and hedges of thorn bushes and roses. When both man and nature were hostile, the defence of gardens by secure walls or other methods of enclosure was essential, and attention is paid to this in written and drawn descriptions. In the illustrations to the *Roman de la Rose* we can find examples of such enclosure varying from rudimentary to sophisticated. A woodcut of about 1481 shows the lover holding up his rose in a small, bare enclosure circled by a woven wattle fence. In 1494 he is less crudely drawn, the rose is more obviously a rose, and the garden fence is of wooden palings, entered by a paling gate with a little tiled roof over it. A far more elaborate, coloured illustration dated about 1475 shows a very detailed idea of an ideal late mediaeval garden. The whole is enclosed by a sturdy, castellated stone wall. Its solid timber door has a heavy iron lock.

Emilià in the garden, seated on a turf bench in front of a rose-clad trellis. French medieval illustration to a story by Boccaccio.

In Britain the stability which followed the end of the Wars of the Roses with the uniting of the red and white roses to form the 'Tudor Rose' allowed the rich and powerful to develop more and more elaborate gardens. In 1533 the Mount at Hampton Court was constructed with a spiral path 'like the turnings of cockle shells' leading up through flower beds edged with green and white rails and planted with evergreens (bay, cypress, holly, juniper and yew) and four hundred roses.

From this time onwards, pamphlets and books of advice to gardeners began to be published. Those that have survived over the centuries include Thomas Tusser's *Hundreth Good Pointes of Husbandrie* (1557), which gives practical advice on the cultivation of vegetables and herbs in rhyming couplets; *The Gardener's Labyrinth* by Thomas Hill (1571); John Gerard's *Herbal*

19

(1597); Gervase Markham's two books, *The English Husbandman* (1613) and *Cheap and Good Husbandry* (1614); William Lawson's *A New Orchard and Garden* and *The Country Housewife's Garden* (both published in 1618); and John Parkinson's *Paradisi in Sole Paradisus Terrestris* (1629). They give a fascinating picture of gardening practice and of the layout of gardens, large and small. As far as roses are concerned, these books are chiefly of interest for their inclusion of roses in lists of plants. Little is said about their ornamental use, but their medicinal qualities are described and recipes are given for rose preserves, jellies and syrups. Thomas Tusser offers advice for ground cover under roses, which I have seen still being followed today:

> *The gooseberry, respis and roses all three*
> *With strawberries under them trimly agree.*

Tusser is talking about the little wild strawberries, *Fragaria vesca*: the fat juicy monsters that we grow now did not exist in his day.

Although most of this early gardening literature is concerned with the medicinal and culinary uses of plants, and the giving of practical horticultural advice, Gerard has this to say about the rose:

> *Though it be a shrub full of prickles, yet it had been more fit and convenient to have placed it with the most glorious floures of the world than to insert the same here among base and thorny shrubs: for the rose does deserve the chief and prime place among all floures whatsoever ... divers of them are high and tall, others short and low ... some be red, others white, and most of them or all sweetly smelling.*

Gerard names fourteen kinds of rose and Parkinson adds another ten. Sir Thomas Hanmer, who gardened in Flintshire, and completed his 'Garden Book' in 1659 (though it was not published until 1933), describes twenty-one roses, including the yellow and scarlet single rose (*R. foetida bicolor*), the velvet rose, the purple rose ('very double and scarce'), the purple striped with white, the marbled rose, 'Rosa Mundi', the Cinnamon rose and the double yellow rose (*R. hemisphaerica*).

We also have records of the roses grown at Ely Place during the reign of Elizabeth I. Ely Place was the London residence of the Bishops of Ely; Queen Elizabeth let the gatehouse to Sir Christopher Hatton for the rent not of a peppercorn but a single

An illustration from Gerard's *Herbal* (1597).

red rose. The garden was famous for its roses and the Bishop was allowed to take twenty bushels of them a year. The roses grown were the double red *R. gallica*, *R. alba*, *R. centifolia*, Damask roses, 'Rosa Mundi', the Musk rose, and the Cinnamon rose.

Today a fine example of a Tudor knot garden can be seen at Hatfield in Hertfordshire. The gardens are laid out to be in keeping with the history of the house which was built by Robert Cecil, first Earl of Salisbury, in 1611. Roses are everywhere including hedges of Sweet briar roses which were much used for their scented leaves from early medieval times onwards. The knot garden has been constructed in the courtyard of the remaining wing of the fifteenth-century Palace of Hatfield, where Queen Elizabeth spent much of her youth, and the atmosphere there evokes her times in the most romantic way. The knot can, as was customary, be viewed from above, so that its pattern is clearly seen. The view is from a shady upper walk beneath a tunnel of pleached limes. The rectangular plot is enclosed by clipped thorn hedges and quartered by gravelled paths with a circular pool in the centre. A brick paved path runs round the perimeter. One quarter is planted in a maze pattern of low, clipped box; the other three are a mass of roses in June and early July, all varieties that were available in the sixteenth century, spilling out of the confines of their box-edged beds and interplanted with herbs and perennials of appropriate date. Arbours provide shade above seats at the sides of the garden.

We usually think of the eighteenth-century Landscape Movement as sounding the death-knell of flowers (and roses among them) in the garden, but the truth is that flowers began to disappear from the gardens of the rich and powerful much earlier. From the Tudor period onwards, gardens became more and more architectural and less and less floriferous. The fashion was for elaborate timber work, including carved and brightly painted animal shapes and fantastical topiary. The ever more convoluted knots and parterres of clipped evergreens left no room for flowers. Their interstices were filled instead with coloured sands and gravels and coal and brick dust. Unruly flowering plants have no place in geometrical extravaganzas, and only those roses that could easily be tamed and trained to cover arbours and alleys or set as dense hedges were of use in the grand formal gardens of the period.

Such fashionable gardens of topiary, knots and carved animals were the natural habitat of Francis Bacon who brought his great intellect to bear on the subject in his essay 'of Gardens' in 1625. Bacon is generally regarded as the prophet of the landscape movement and was contemptuous of much of what he saw in contemporary gardens: 'As for the making of knots or figures with divers coloured earths, they be but toys; you may see as good sights many times in tarts ... images cut in juniper or other garden stuff; they be for children.'

If Bacon had intimations of informality, a century was still to pass before Shaftesbury, Addison and Pope formulated the philosophy of landscape and Bridgeman and Kent, and later Brown and Repton, began to practise it. Nature would reign supreme for close to another hundred years. During this time the craft of gardening would take second place to the art of landscaping and roses would be relegated to the walled flower garden, away from the house.

But roses are not quite without their place in the 'natural' garden. Among twenty-six shrubs recommended by Batty Langley in *New Principles of Gardening* (1728) for planting in 'the Wilderness', no fewer than eight are roses: 'Cinnamon, Damask, Cabbage, "Rosa Mundi", White Musk, Red Rose, Yellow Rose, Sweet Briar.' Langley recommends that they should be 'planted promiscuously ... not in regular lines, as has been the common Way. But, on the contrary, in little Thickets, or Clusters, seemingly without any other Order than what Nature directed, which, of all others, is the most beautiful.'

The philosophy of landscape held the imagination of thoughtful landowners until inevitably a time for change arrived. Claudian landscapes, horrid grottoes, sublime gorges, Gothick ruins: none of these could satisfy permanently the desire inherent in man to grow plants which celebrate the beauty of flowers.

This desire was stimulated by the great wealth of trees, shrubs and other plants being introduced to Europe from other continents. There was also, perhaps, a social reason for the return to ornamental gardening: the rise of a prosperous middle class. After all you cannot make an impressive landscape behind a Georgian terraced house or in the few acres attached to a merchant's suburban seat. A new kind of gardening was needed and one of the elements that came to fulfill the need was the rosary, rosarium or rose garden.

Above Charles I with Alba roses: window in the Hall of Magdalen College, Oxford.

Right 'June', from Robert Furber's *Twelve Months of Flowers*, 1730. engraving by H. Fletcher from a painting by Pieter Casteels.

1 Perennial dwarf Sun flower.
  Ultamarine & Prusian blew
2 Iris Major.
  Blew Nigella.
3   or Fennel flower.
4 Moon Trefoile.
5 Upright Sweet William.
6 Saxifrage.
7 Cinque foile.

8 Pansies, or Hearts-ease.
9 Maidens blush Rose.
10 Yellow Jasmine.
11 Blew Corn flower.
12 Blush Belgick Rose.
13 The Francford Rose.
14 Double Martagon.
15 Orchis or Bee flower.
16 Scarlet Colutea.

17 Fraxinella.
18 Moss province Rose.
19 Double Virginian Silk-grass.
20 White Rose.
21 Dutch Hundred Leav'd Rose.
22 White Batchelors Button.
23 Rosa Mundi.
24 Mountain Lychnis.
25 Dwarf Iris Strip'd.

26 White Jasmine.
27 Scarlet Geranium.
28 Yellow Martagon.
29 Red Martagon.
30 Teucrium or Germander.
31 Mountain dwarf Pink.
32 Yellow Corn Mary gold.
33 Purple sweet Pea.
34 Greek Valerian.

JUNE

Design'd by P.r Casteels.

From the Collection of Rob.t Furber, Gardiner at Kensington. 1730.

Engrav'd by H. Fletcher.

CHAPTER THREE

An Empress and her Roses

Le Rosier est de beaucoup le plus important de tous les arbustes cultivés pour l'ornament des jardins.

M. Cochet-Cochet, *Les Rosiers*, 1896

In 1799 Josephine Bonaparte bought the château of Malmaison near Choisy with its estate of 650 acres, while Napoleon was away fighting his Egyptian campaign.

In England we are rather possessive about the rose. It is our national flower; beautiful girls have complexions like English roses. 'Unkempt about our hedges blows' Rupert Brooke's 'English, unofficial rose'. We also tend to think of rose gardens as a particularly English form which we have exported to the fortunate rest of the world. The fact is that France has a better claim to be the cradle of the rose, and to have invented the rose garden. The French are certainly as much a nation of rose-lovers today as any other, including the English. Driving through France in June, one is overwhelmed by roses. Even houses without gardens have their balconies wreathed in roses which appear to have been planted directly into the tarmac or cobbles of the road, and every town of any size has its *roseraie* to embellish a corner of the municipal park. And we owe the idea of the *roseraie* to a French woman who was, so far as we can tell, the first rose enthusiast to make a collection of roses and set them apart in a garden of their own. Indeed, Josephine's *roseraie* was the first garden ever to be devoted to a single genus.

It is appropriate that the first rose garden should have been made in France. The influence of the Romans was more wide-spread in France than in England: Gaul was an immediate neighbour, accessible by land, with a more friendly climate than the cold, damp, foggy weather that made Julius Caesar's army so homesick when in Britain. It is likely that Roman governors there would have built villas not unlike the one described by Pliny, although perhaps on a more modest scale. It was at Bordeaux that the Roman poet Ausonius wrote of watching the sunset from the rose garden of his villa.

Evidence of the structure and planting of medieval gardens

'La Rose de la Malmaison' by J. L. Viger du Vigneau, 1867.

comes mainly from French and Flemish sources, such as the exquisite miniatures by Pol de Limbourg in the *Très Riches Heures du duc de Berry* (1409–16). There are also records of the extensive gardens created by Charles VI in 1398 at the Hôtel de St Pol in Paris. Gardens of the imagination flourished too. In the *Seconde Semaine*, a poem on the Creation, du Bartas writes of the Garden of Eden. A translation by Joshua Sylvester describes Adam walking in a rose garden which 'the Angels did daily dresse in true love-knots, tri-angles and lozenges.'

There were few rose gardens outside the imaginations of poets during the seventeenth and eighteenth centuries, when French garden design was developing into the supreme example of the triumph of art over nature, and this on the grandest scale, reaching its spectacular climax at Versailles. It was after the death of Louis XIV in 1715 that French taste began to react against extreme formality, and *jardins à l'anglaise*, as the French described their interpretations of the landscape style, began to be fashionable.

Josephine commissioned Louis Berthault to make just such a garden at Malmaison. His informal landscape contained a lake fed by a winding stream with cascades and spanned by graceful

Above The Château and part of the gardens at Malmaison.

Right Malmaison today.

26

bridges, a *Temple d'Amour* set on a rocky mound, statuary, and a fine collection of trees and shrubs from all over the world. Today only five hectares of the garden and mere fragments of the original planting remain.

During the first years Napoleon was First Consul and his official residence was the Tuileries. But he was a frequent visitor at Malmaison where life was informal and relaxed. His visits ceased after his coronation as Emperor in 1804, but Josephine continued to use the château whenever she was able and, after her divorce in 1810, lived there permanently until her death on 29 May 1814, apparently from a cold caught during a reception given for Tsar Alexander I a few days earlier. She loved the place and was passionately interested in its garden.

During her comparatively short life (she was fifty when she died) Josephine was gay, charming, elegant and, fortunately for the future of roses and rose gardens, extremely extravagant. Because of her position, money was not a problem when forming her collection of rare plants and she was able to command the services of many eminent botanists, among them Etienne-Pierre Ventenat, Charles-François Brisseau de Mirbel and André Thouin.

Her aim, which was indeed ambitious, was to assemble every known variety of rose from every part of the world at Malmaison. The task had recently become more difficult, but very much more exciting, by the introduction to Europe of three roses of key importance for future hybridising: 'Slater's Crimson China' was brought from China in about 1792 by Gilbert Slater of Leytonstone; 'Parson's Pink China' was noticed in Parson's garden at Rickmansworth in 1793, and may have been collected in China by Sir George Staunton the previous year; 'Hume's Blush Tea-scented China' was probably discovered in 1809, also in China, by Sir A. Hume, Bart. (There was a fourth, 'Parks's Yellow Tea-scented China', which I mention here for convenience, although it was not known until ten years after Josephine's death.)

The significance of these four roses was their ability to produce flowers continuously from May to October, whereas hitherto all roses had a fleeting moment of glory lasting just for a few weeks in June, with the exception of the Autumn Damask of Samos and Paestum which, as its name implies, produces a second crop in the autumn. Graham Stuart Thomas in *The Old Shrub Roses*

gives an account of the revolutionary effect these four new intro-
ductions had upon rose breeding. They are parents or ancestors
of the Noisette rose, the Bourbon, the Tea rose, Hybrid Chinas,
Hybrid Perpetuals, Hybrid Teas, Polypompons, and most
modern roses.

All four of the 'Stud Chinas' reached France quickly: indeed
such was the urgency in the case of 'Hume's Blush China' that
the British and French navies arranged safe conduct for the ship
that was carrying it to Malmaison during the height of hostilities
between the two countries. The Napoleonic Wars were not interrupted for every rose grower, however. In 1815, as the Allies
were preparing to march into Paris, Vibert, a distinguished rose
grower and breeder had to rescue 10,000 seedlings from Descemet's nursery at St. Denis and rush them to safety on the Marne.
According to Catherine Frances Gore, in her book *The Book of
Roses* (1838), poor M. Descemet was 'cut up by the English
troops'. Fortunately he was able to proceed to Russia and re-
establish himself 'with honour and success.'

The Empress had a close rival in the collecting of rare plants
and roses in the Comtesse de Bougainville. The competition not
only added impetus to the efforts of both ladies, but helped to
develop an interest in roses and rose gardens in fashionable circles
that was to last well into the twentieth century.

To her other resources Josephine was able to add the skills of
an Englishman, Mr Kennedy of the partnership of Kennedy and
Lee, nurserymen trading at Hammersmith, who joined forces in
the world-wide search for roses with M. André du Pont, the
director of the Jardins de Luxembourg in Paris where he established another famous collection of roses.

The Luxembourg Rose Garden was established in a sunken
rectangle to be viewed from an upper walk. The simple layout
of long rectangular beds in rows was framed by a line of fruit
trees round the outer beds. The rose breeder Eugène Hardy, who
was du Pont's successor at the Jardins de Luxembourg, also served
Malmaison well. Later in his career, in 1832, he produced and
named after his wife the rose which Graham Stuart Thomas refers
to as 'the incomparable white hybrid Damask Rose "Madame
Hardy"'. Still, after 150 years, incomparable; I wish the Empress
could have seen it. I wish, too, that she could have seen that
other very lovely rose, 'Souvenir de la Malmaison', which was

Tea rose from *Les Roses*, vol. I,
by Pierre-Joseph Redouté, 1817.

28

Rosa Indica fragrans.   *Rosier des Indes odorant.*

(*vulg Bengale à odeur de thé.*)

P. J. Redouté pinx.   Imprimerie de Remond   Langlois sculp.

sent to Malmaison in about 1843 and given its wistful name by
a Grand Duke of Russia who visited Malmaison in search of roses
for the imperial garden at St. Petersburg.

One of the many favours which Josephine bestowed on a
posterity of rose lovers was her appointment of the most famous
botanical artist ever, Pierre-Joseph Redouté, to make pictorial
records of her plants. He made coloured drawings of 117 of the
rose varieties at Malmaison, and his careful observation, meticulously accurate drawing and delicate, truthful colouring have
been of great help to later rose scholars in identifying old-
fashioned roses lost and rediscovered. If we now tend to take
Redouté's drawings for granted, that is because their popularity
has been so great. We have become used to seeing reproductions
of them framed and hung in so many hotel rooms and spare
bedrooms that familiarity has bred boredom.

Redouté was a botanist as well as an artist, which partly
accounts for the accuracy of his drawings. He and Thory, the
distinguished botanist who wrote the text describing the roses in
Redouté's book, started breeding experiments with 'Slater's
Crimson China' in 1798, soon after the rose arrived in France.

With such a fine team at work, and such an energetic and
enthusiastic woman directing them, what sort of rose garden was
there at Malmaison? Sadly, it gradually fell into disrepair after
Josephine died, along with the rest of the gardens, so no traces
of the original *roseraie* survive. Two drawings exist of the gardens
dated 1806 and 1815: the latter, made after the death of Josephine
for Prince Eugène, shows a formal layout in the pattern of a
Union Jack. It is not known whether these symmetrical beds were
planted with roses, but this was the design chosen in 1983 for a
project to restore the Empress's roses to Malmaison. To date,
with the help of experts in Europe and from as far afield as
Australia, 110 varieties have been located and 800 bushes planted
to represent them.

It is sad to think that Josephine did not live to see more of the
results of her patronage of the rose. It was really only after her
death that new hybrids, many of them with a long flowering
season, began to be produced in astounding variety of colour
and form. At the end of the previous century, Diderot had listed
eighty varieties of rose, of which a third had single flowers.
Josephine more than doubled this number, growing 167 Gallica

roses, twenty-seven Centifolias, twenty-two Chinas, nine Damasks, eight Albas, four Spinosissimas, three luteas, *R. moschata*, *R. carolina* and *R. setigera*. By 1829 Desportes, in the *Rosetum Gallicum*, names 2,500 roses. Even allowing that many may have been hardly distinct from one another, and others may have proved unsatisfactory in some way, that is still *embarras de richesse* by any standards.

Malmaison was the forerunner of many elegant rose gardens in France: these are epitomised by two relatively early examples, both near Paris, both little altered since their construction, and both immaculately cared for today. One is in the park of the Château de Bagatelle in the Bois de Boulogne in Paris; the other is the *roseraie* at l'Haÿ-les-Roses, a suburb to the south-west. Both are easily accessible from the capital and, even in mid-June, when the display is at its most splendid, they are not too crowded. (Admittedly the days when I visited them were very wet days in mid-June.) They illustrate perfectly the French ideal of a rose garden. Both hold collections which form an invaluable reservoir of historic and rare roses used by rose scholars and rose breeders from all over the world but, more than collections, they are gardens of rare and spectacular beauty to be enjoyed by everyone.

The *roseraie* at l'Haÿ predates Bagatelle by just four years. In 1892 Jules Gravereaux, owner of the department store Bon Marché, bought the property at l'Haÿ on his retirement and set about indulging his passion for roses. It brought him into contact with collectors and botanical gardens all over the world, and he assembled an extensive collection of species and hybrid roses. The collection began to outgrow its allotted space and, in 1899, he commissioned the landscape architect Edouard André to design a special garden for the roses.

Gravereaux's ambition was to have the finest collection in the world and to show the many various forms of rose bush displayed in as many different ways as they could be. By 1900 he was growing three thousand different varieties of rose. His house as well as his garden was full of roses and images of roses. He had his office and his laboratory in a building in the centre of the rose garden where he also kept an ever-increasing collection of arts and crafts inspired by, or depicting roses: books, paintings, drawings, sculptures, textiles, pottery and porcelain, ivories, stamps and coins. Sadly, this irreplaceable collection was stolen in 1980.

The garden that André laid out at l'Haÿ is on level ground. It is a more or less right-angled triangle, shaped into a giant fan decorated with a central medallion consisting of a pool surrounded by a parterre of lawns and bedding roses. The main axis leads past the pool and up a broad flight of steps to an imposing trellised pavilion with pergola wings on either side while, on both sides of the central medallion, paths fan out from the Norman pavilion to the boundaries. The spaces thus created are further divided and subdivided by a network of subsidiary paths.

The overall plan is reminiscent of the grand formal gardens of seventeenth-century France, writ small and coloured exuberantly. Each compartment is treated differently, to demonstrate its own botanical or historical theme. There is 'La Roseraie de Madame' showing the best roses to use as cut flowers; L'Allée Historique de la Rose, which shows the evolution of roses from wild species to modern hybrids; Les Roses de la Malmaison, planted with Josephine's roses, and other separate little gardens for the botanical collection, for Gallica roses, for the roses of Asia (Species and hybrids), for 'modern' (1850–1950) varieties no longer commercially available, for the best foreign roses, for new French roses, for tea-scented roses, and for Rugosa and *pimpinellifolia* roses.

Do not imagine that the didactic purpose of these divisions detracts from their decorative qualities. When you enter the garden you find yourself embraced by fragrance and overwhelmed with rich and diverse colours even on the dullest day. The use of colour is uninhibited, neon-orange 'Super Star' and egg-yolk 'Sutter's Gold' jostling crimsons and reds such as 'Etoile de Hollande' and 'Chrysler Imperial'. Such is the kaleidoscopic exuberance of the garden viewed overall that it does not occur to you to quarrel with individual juxtapositions which, at home, might make the fastidious disciple of good taste wince a little. Moreover, when sated with colour, you can move from an area of brilliant display to a quieter place and contemplate the gentle charm of the evocatively named Alba roses: 'Céleste', 'Rosée du Matin' and 'Cuisse de Nymphe' ('Maiden's Blush'). You can move away from the brightness of the reds, yellows and oranges into one of the tunnelled walks dressed with ramblers with their luxuriant, dark, glossy leaves. There is every pleasure here that roses can give, from massed colour to single perfect blooms, with a range

Above Roses immaculately trained on tall iron tripods at Roseraie de l'Haÿ near Paris.

Right The rambler 'Alexandre Girault' smothers the trellised pergola and pavilion at l'Haÿ-les-Roses.

that embraces the sweet simplicity of *R. canina* (the dog rose), the velvety richness of 'Charles de Mills' with its flat, full, quartered flower, and the flawless miniature buds of 'Cécile Brunner'.

Apart from the general plan of the garden, and from the roses themselves, I would single out three things which particularly contribute to its beauty. All three are of the utmost importance in the design of gardens in general. The first is the background to the garden. It is bounded by walls, mostly concealed to a great extent by wide-meshed square trellis supporting climbing roses, but the significant background is in the park outside the boundaries. The *roseraie* at l'Haÿ has the good fortune to be encircled by mature forest trees, providing a high, dense background of quiet green to offset the colour within.

The second factor is the careful attention that has been paid to the vertical element, which is often insufficiently considered in gardens, particularly in rose gardens. Here, vertical features that are in scale with the garden as a whole are provided by roses. Indeed, apart from immaculately clipped box edgings to the beds and areas of lawn, there are no other plants in the garden but roses. The graceful, flattened arches that span the shady walks and which support climbers and ramblers, are some 8 ft/2·5m high with a generous span of 13 ft/4m. Other vigorous climbers are spectacularly displayed on tall, narrow iron pyramids, with four plants to each, and in other parts of the garden a different atmosphere is evoked by the use of rustic timber structures of varying heights.

Elsewhere, punctuating the beds and borders at an intermediate height are standard roses. I do not generally care much for ordinary standards – they too often resemble much-used lavatory brushes with their scrawny little heads on long sticks. But at l'Haÿ-les-Roses they are so well grown and well presented that I could almost be converted. The heads are dense, shapely and well-clothed with foliage and flowers and of a size that is in proportion to the stem. But I still do not like to see a plant held up by a stick, whether it is a rose or a delphinium.

Weeping standards are a different matter. Falling from a height of some 7 ft/2m they display their flexible, flower-smothered wands with grace and elegance. Among the loveliest at l'Haÿ are 'New Dawn', 'Paul Noël', 'Aviateur Blériot', 'Romeo', 'Excelsa' and 'Neige d'Avril'. Apart from 'New Dawn', none of them is

34

familiar today in Britain, though Peter Beales lists 'Aviateur Blériot' and 'Excelsa' in his catalogue.

Skill in training plants to perform as they are required to is one of the things that sets French rose gardens apart. The bold and free use of colour is contained by strict discipline and restraint in the mode of growth. It is not always pleasing to see plants used as the raw material of architecture or decoration, clipped or twisted to suit the designer; but here, severe pruning and training succeeds in creating spectacularly elegant, theatrical effects.

The third general design principle that I noted at the Roseraie de l'Haÿ was the use of bold blocks of massed colour to relieve the restless, kaleidoscopic effect of many colours mixed at random. The core of the garden illustrates this principle: the orderly symmetry of pool and lawns is augmented with beds of massed Floribunda and Hybrid Tea roses. The oval shape of this central area is bounded by tall pillars of 'Paul's Scarlet Climber' alternating with 'Mrs F.W. Flight', and the grand climax is the closing of the main vista with the magnificent trellised pavilion, its arcades curving out to embrace the garden. The temptation to use this large structure to display a wide variety of roses has been resisted: its whole length is covered with just one variety, the coppery pink rambler 'Alexandre Girault'. Although it flowers only in June, the foliage is luxuriant and glossy, forming dark green architecture for the rest of the season. It is strongly scented and the whole effect is unforgettable.

M. Gravereaux was also instrumental in the creation of the other great Parisian rose garden at the Bagatelle in the Bois de Boulogne. In 1906 he provided several hundred different species and varieties of rose for this garden, then being created by Jean-Claude Nicolas Forestier who was in charge of landscaping the Bois.

At this time the château de Bagatelle was owned by the City of Paris, after a varied and colourful history and many changes of ownership. From 1720 to 1745 the maréchale d'Estrées, '*fort jolie, fort séduisante et fort peu farouche*', made the château a discreet meeting place for aristocratic lovers, including the young king Louis XV. She was followed by another aristocratic 'Madame' in the marquise de Monconseil who also included Louis XV among her clients; the marquise was such an extravagant party-

giver that she became unable to afford the upkeep of the little château and it fell into disrepair.

Eventually, in 1775, the ruin that remained became the property of the comte d'Artois. The count was a passionate gambler and accepted a bet with his sister-in-law, Marie-Antoinette, that he could not rebuild the château in two months. Nine hundred workers toiled day and night for him to win the bet, and the result is the château which we see today. He carried out equally dashing alterations to the park, employing the Scottish landscaper, Thomas Blaikie, to make a garden in the new English picturesque style. This was one of the earliest French gardens to show reaction against the grand formality of Le Nôtre's style.

After the Revolution the château changed hands several times, including a period in Napoleon's ownership, and was bought in 1835 by the English Marquess of Hertford. Lord Hertford built the Orangery and levelled the area below it to make a riding school for the young Imperial Prince. On a slope to the east he placed a little summer house in the form of an oriental kiosk where the Empress Eugénie could sit and watch the Prince's riding lessons. Today the riding school is the *roseraie* and the Empress's kiosk marks its focal point.

Lord Hertford died at Bagatelle in 1870, leaving the property to his adopted son Sir Richard Wallace. A francophile and a connoisseur of the arts, Sir Richard is remembered in England as the donor to the nation of the Wallace Collection; one hopes in France he is still remembered occasionally for his gift of a hundred fountains to the city of Paris. He, too, died at Bagatelle.

It was Forestier's idea that the city should acquire the château and its park from Wallace's heirs. The arrangement was completed in January 1905, and the *roseraie* was planted the following year. More intimate than that at l'Haÿ (it occupies an area of about 120 sq yd/100 sq m by 90 sq yd/75 sq m), Bagatelle's *roseraie* shows the same combination of elegance, exuberance and romance. It accommodates a similar variety of roses, old and modern, bush and climbing, species and hybrids, having altogether some 8,000 roses in 700 varieties. The International Exhibition of New Roses has been held annually at Bagatelle since 1907.

As at l'Haÿ, the background is wooded, with distant views beyond the trees from the vantage point of the Empress's kiosk.

Above A formal pattern of beds, pillars and pergolas in the Roseraie at la Bagatelle.

Below The bush roses at la Bagatelle are planted in box-edged turf beds.

From the kiosk too one can appreciate the orderly, symmetrical layout of the box-edged beds, punctuated at key points by the solid geometry of tall, immaculately clipped cones of yew. The beds are carpeted with turf, with neat circles cut out for each rose bush. Simple timber pergolas cover the walks, raised higher to form arbours where two walks cross. Ropes and chains bound with thick twine are slung between unpeeled rustic poles to form swags and festoons of climbing and rambling roses, and horizontal poles or chains carry rose friezes knee-high, waist-high and shoulder-high.

I have visited Bagatelle in March when it was instructive to see the skeleton which would be fleshed out with roses later in the year. Each climbing rose was restricted to a few strong stems, ruthlessly bent to follow the direction required and firmly secured at frequent intervals with twisted twigs, presumably the pruned shoots from the roses. The use of flexible twigs to tie in the stems must be traditional and is an attractive alternative to modern wire or plastic ties. The winter heads of standard roses were little stumps with not more than half a dozen shoots, each a few inches long. Climbers on tall metal tripods were bent around the support in a spiral. It is an object-lesson to gardeners who cannot achieve

Left The winter skeleton of the *roseraie* at Bagatelle (compare with the summer view on p. 36).

Right Bagatelle: Ramblers trained at different heights on swags and pergolas.

the results they would like because they are too tender-hearted towards their plants. In the midst of this rather harsh scene, under a persistent fine drizzle of rain, a peacock was unfurling his flamboyant tail with a swaggering confidence that he would surely cease to feel in June when the roses would be bidding to eclipse him.

There is another *roseraie* of great charm in Paris, of a very different character. The Jardin Albert Kahn can be entered from 1 Rue des Abondances or from 9 Quai du 4 Septembre. Laid out by the philanthropist and political philosopher Albert Kahn between 1894 and 1911, the garden is now owned by the local authority. In a comparatively small space (300 sq yd/250 sq m by 230 sq yd/200 sq m) beside the Seine, Kahn created eight separate gardens, including an English Garden, a Japanese Garden, and three 'forests'.

One of Kahn's gardens was the Jardin Fruitier et Roseraie. Perhaps in making it he recalled his birthplace in Alsace or his later home at Boulogne. At any rate, this dear little garden has a provincial rather than Parisian atmosphere. In a simple framework of grassed rectangles with central circular beds, apples, pears, plums, mulberries and peaches are trained as distaffs, spindles (this is a literal translation from the French), goblets, espaliers and cordons. A walk runs the length of the garden spanned by arches clothed in scented roses in different shades of pink, all with a bluish tinge and all underplanted with a carpet of purple alyssum. It seems like a rustic oasis in the middle of Paris, that most urbane of cities.

In any part of France it is worth looking out for rose gardens and exciting to come upon one unexpectedly. In Bourges we came upon one in the Prés Fischaux gardens while waiting for the cathedral to open after lunch (worth the wait, even without the rose garden). A long rectangular lawn is bordered with wide, very slender yew arches. The roses are trained on tall tripods and on globes fashioned from metal rods.

The garden at Bourges and countless other modern municipal gardens throughout France are in the classic French tradition of l'Haÿ and Bagatelle. Like many of the best traditions, it continues to be followed because it continues to please.

CHAPTER FOUR

Rich Man, Poor Man

*Queen Rose is far too haughty a monarch to allow the common herd
of garden plants to approach too closely . . . Air and sunshine cir-
culating freely through all the branches are essential to success.*

Walter P. Wright *Roses and Rose Gardens* (1911)

The exchange of information, ideas and plants between English
and French rose enthusiasts and professional nurserymen continued despite the Napoleonic Wars and increased after hostilities
had ended.

The development of new rose hybrids coincided with a change
of taste. The 'natural' landscaped gardens of the eighteenth
century were hardly gardens at all, if a garden is a place set apart
for the cultivation of flowering plants, and there was an increasing need for space to display the booty of plant-hunters who were
making exciting discoveries all over the world. There was also a
reaction against the dullness of much of the landscaping. The
Revd William Mason (1725–97) was an early critic of stan-
dardised landscape design and a persuasive advocate of flower
gardens. He used roses liberally even before the break-through in
rose breeding. His garden designs showed an informality which
in many ways bridges the gap between the ideas of Bacon 150
years earlier and those of William Robinson and Gertrude Jekyll
100 years later. He was influenced by the ideas of Jean-Jacques
Rousseau and based his major work at Nuneham Park near
Oxford on Julie's garden in Rousseau's novel *La Nouvelle
Héloïse*. His friend Lord Nuneham, later the first Earl of Harcourt,
commissioned Mason to design a flower garden, of which an
excellent record remains in a painting by Paul Sandby.

The planting at Nuneham Park illustrates not only a new feeling
for informality in the flower garden, but also a yearning for
colour, scent and beauty of flower that roses were well qualified
to satisfy. They were soon being used both formally in mixed
flower gardens and informally in shrubberies. For example, in
1790 Humphrey Repton used roses and honeysuckles in the
shrubbery walks at Langley Park in Kent.

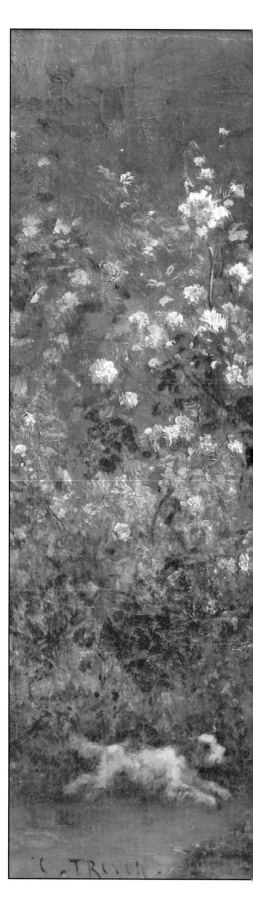

'A Walk in the Rose Garden' by Constant Tryon (1810–1865).

Formality near the house was increasingly felt to be more appropriate that the Brownian idea of sheep grazing up to the windows and, when the French fashion for separate rose gardens arrived in England, their design began by following the French pattern of theatrical display in a formal setting. Early examples can be seen in Repton's designs for rosaries at Woburn Abbey (1804) and at Ashridge in Hertfordshire (1816).

To satisfy an increasing demand, specialist rose nurseries were springing up in England, A. Paul and Son at Cheshunt (founded in 1806) and Thomas Rivers at Sawbridgeworth being prominent among them. By 1836 Rivers was offering 700 varieties, one third of which were available as standards.

From the design point of view, it is interesting to see that Rivers recommends using the more vigorous *R. sempervirens* varieties as undergrowth in wildernesses near the pleasure-ground, thus pre-empting William Robinson and Gertrude Jekyll by half a century, and also recognising that many roses which were then (and still are today) usually trained to grow upwards are more naturally prostrate colonisers. He also recommends the dwarf China roses, sometimes known as 'fairy roses' for use on rock-work.

It was not long before Rivers and William Paul were publishing books on rose cultivation and the choice of varieties for different uses in the garden. Rivers' *The Rose Amateur's Guide* came out in 1837 and it was followed a year later by one of the first of many books about roses written by keen and knowledgeable amateurs. Catherine Frances Gore's *The Book of Roses or The Rose Fancier's Manual* was mainly derived from M. Paul Boitard's *Manuel complet de l'Amateur de Rose*, published in Paris in 1836. Mrs Gore seems to have been endowed with great energy. Born in 1799, she married at the age of twenty-four and had ten children. The rose book was a departure from her usual subject: she was really a writer of fiction, and published seventy novels, many of them in three volumes. Her *Book of Roses* describes 1,432 varieties, and mentions rose gardens she has visited in France and England, including four which she considers the best: they are that of the Horticultural Society (later the Royal Horticultural Society) under Professor Lindley at Chiswick, the Duke of Devonshire's under Paxton, Mr Joseph Sabine's at North Mimms and Mr Charles James Fox's at St Anne's Hill. Mrs Gore

Two plates from Humphrey Repton's *Fragments on the Theory and Practice of Landscape Gardening* (1816).

Above 'View From My Own Cottage in Essex'.

Right 'The Rosary at Ashbridge'.

writes with confidence and conviction about roses throughout the world, stating with relish that 'In vast thickets of the beautiful *Rosa semperflorens* the tigers of Bengal and crocodiles of the Ganges are known to wait for their prey.'

William Paul's *The Rose Garden* (1848) is of particular interest for the information and advice it offers on the design and layout of rose gardens, and for a list he gives of names and addresses of rose amateurs with whom he was in correspondence. It is pleasing that, as well as the owner, he often mentions the gardener by name. Like Mrs Gore, Paul mentions Mr Sabine's collection at

South Mimms where he specialised in Species roses. Sabine was an energetic and effective Secretary of the Horticultural Society from 1816 to 1830 when he was forced to resign because of embezzlement by his assistant. Among the gardeners who corresponded with Paul were Mr W. Ingram at Hatfield, Mr M'Intosh at Dalkeith and Mr Ruffett at Brockett Hall.

His advice on the layout of rose gardens (which we may assume was widely followed since, then as now, owners frequently called in a nurseryman to design their gardens) was to keep the form of the beds simple and geometric: squares, circles, ovals and other regular figures would be in harmony with the character of the roses. He thought that plain grass paths made the best setting to display the roses but that, if gravel was insisted upon, the beds should be edged with box, or slate or fancy tiles or with more roses, fairy or pompon. In Mr George Bosanquet's garden at Broxbournebury, Hertfordshire, which Paul describes and illustrates with a plan, the edging is of white coated flintstones, six inches apart, planted with sedums and other rock plants.

Mr Paul recommended having a raised mound thrown up in the centre of the rose garden, or at one end, to provide a bird's eye view of the garden. The mound would be planted with Ayrshire and Sempervirens roses and crowned with a rose temple or with a cluster of pillar roses. He recommended defining the boundary with a single row of pillar roses a yard apart, or pillars at two yards with chains slung between them on which to train festoons of roses, or else a rustic fence planted with Bourbon, Noisette or Sweetbriar roses.

Rose beds, Paul advises, may be planted either in mixed colours or with each colour massed separately. He describes the rose walk at Southgate House, seat of Isaac Walker, Esq., where, on a strip of land taken from the park, a single row of beds is cut comprising circles, segments, octagons and ovals. The roses are planted in botanical groups, Bourbons nearest the house, then French roses, Provence roses, Damasks, Perpetuals, Moss roses, Chinas and so on.

Despite Miss Jekyll's strictures, the remnants of Paul's circles, segments, octagons and ovals can still be seen in many a garden, and many new gardens are still being laid out in this fashion. It is much rarer to find an example today of the more elaborate rose gardens of this period: those with pillars, swags and temples.

The rambler 'Débutante' covering one of the arbours in the Victorian Rose Garden at Warwick Castle.

44

The gardens at Warwick Castle.

The fragile structures of timber or iron have long ago rotted or rusted away, and the cost of re-creating them now is prohibitive. But one outstanding example has recently been constructed and planted.

The plan for the rose garden at Warwick Castle was first drawn in 1868 by the landscape gardener Robert Marnock for his client the fourth Earl of Warwick. Marnock's earlier commissions had included Weston Park, Sheffield Botanic Gardens, and the Royal

46

Botanic Society's gardens in the inner circle of Regent's Park in
London. He was considered by some to be the best landscape
designer of his day. The Warwick Castle rose garden disappeared
after the 1930s, but in 1979 his drawing for the layout and a
sketch for some of the ironwork were discovered in the County
Record Office by Paul Edwards, the landscape and garden con-
sultant to the Castle's owners. The quality of the design makes it
of great historical importance, both in terms of garden history
in general, and in terms of the history of the 800-year-old castle
and its grounds. The decision was therefore taken to recreate the
rose garden. Paul Edwards' skilful and accurate interpretation of
Marnock's drawings has resulted in a garden of great beauty,
and we are able to see today an example of all that is best in
Victorian formal gardening.

The setting for the garden is a clearing in Capability Brown's
wooded landscape; the encircling trees provide the necessary
sober background to a scintillating display. The layout is decep-
tively simple. But the apparently simple geometric shapes of the
rose beds, the grass and the gravelled paths are arranged with an
impressive mastery of proportion. This can be appreciated when
seen from above. All gardens which are designed as a pattern on
the ground should have a vantage point from which to enjoy
their symmetry, and this has been provided from a seat at the top
of the newly restored rock garden. the pattern of the beds is
emphasised with edgings of clipped dwarf box or *Ilex crenata*
'Convexa' (a dense, small-leaved dwarf holly).

There are two entrances to the garden: one is through an elegant
and imposing double wrought iron gate, the other through a
walk spanned by twelve double arches planted with the scented,
creamy-flowered rambler 'Albéric Barbier', which flowers spectacularly in June and again, less profusely, later in the season. I
cannot decide whether it is better to approach the garden for the
first time through this delicious tunnel which prepares the visitor
for delights yet to come, or whether it should be treated as the
climax to the visit. On entering the garden one is greeted by
enchanting colours and scents. Symmetrically placed arches,
arbours and tall tripods are clothed in the clusters and trusses of
ramblers in shades of white, cream and soft pink: 'Débutante',
'Adélaïde d'Orléans', 'May Queen', 'Félicité et Perpétue', 'Aimée
Vibert' and 'The Garland'. In the two oval beds, standards of

'Félicité et Perpétue' weep over a carpet of 'Little White Pet', and the round beds are planted with Centifolia 'de Meaux', with three standard 'de Meaux' raised proud above them. Not all the roses used here are authentically Victorian – Paul Edwards has also chosen modern roses which are more reliably healthy and have a longer flowering season – but all are in keeping with the period. The new English roses bred by David Austin to produce continuous flowers of old-fashioned shape and colour on healthy bushes have proved particularly appropriate. The spirit of the garden and the colours of the flowers are completely authentic. There are no yellows, scarlets or oranges. But the pinks range from palest blush to strongest rose pink, and the reds from crimson to the violet-purple of 'Reine des Violettes'. 'Camaieux' and 'Commandant Beaurepaire' represent the Victorian interest in striped roses, and there are Moss roses too.

In due course, as the new roses of the Victorian age became more widely available and less expensive, the passion for them spread from 'the rich man in his castle' to 'the poor man at the gate'. It is not difficult to conjure a romantic image of him at the gate of his rustic thatched cottage wreathed in roses. Cottage gardens were later to become something of a cult, but they only told part of the poor man's story.

The great majority of poor people lived in dirty, smokey, cramped terraces of houses in the expanding new industrial centres of the Midlands and the North. Their gardening had to take place in dark, polluted back yards or on allotments under the shadow of dark, satanic mills. Perhaps a love for the beauty of flowers and an urge to assist in their creation is strengthened in people who have to live in conditions of hardship in dingy surroundings. Perhaps the contrasting miracle of flowering plants becomes a necessity. Certainly near-miracles of horticulture were performed in the most unpromising conditions by miners and factory workers. Mostly they loved and grew the eight 'florists' flowers' (so defined by the Florists' Societies of the time, under whose aegis growers competed in showing their plants): tulip, auricula, carnation, pink, anemone, ranunculus, hyacinth and polyanthus.

The nineteenth century saw the founding of Horticultural Societies throughout Britain, which fostered an interest in gardening among all social classes and disseminated technical expert-

Penstemons, campanulas and foxgloves complement the pinks, whites and purples of old roses at Mottisfont.

48

ise. Interest in, and knowledge of gardening were also spread ever wider by the publication of an increasing number of gardening magazines: in 1841 *The Gardener's Chronicle* founded by Joseph Paxton; in 1848 *The Cottage Gardener*; in 1858 *The Floral World* edited by Shirley Hibberd who also wrote *The Amateur's Rose Book*; and Robinson's *Gardening* (later named *Gardening Illustrated*) in 1879. To cater for an ever wider market, many new nurseries appeared, both general and specialist. By 1910 the Revd A. Foster-Melliar in a new edition of *The Book of the Rose* recommends several rose nurseries in addition to those of Rivers and Paul. They include B. R. Cant and Sons, and Frank Cant and Co., both of Colchester; Prior and Sons, also of Colchester; Turner of Slough; R. Harkness and Co. of Hitchin; Mr Prince of Oxford; A. Dickson and Son of Newtownards in Ireland and also of Ledbury; and Hugh Dickson of Belfast.

The democratisation of gardening through the Horticultural Societies (a system which thrives to this day) led to keen competitiveness among amateur rose-growers as well as professionals. In 1848 William Paul is already giving advice as to which roses make the best specimen blooms for exhibition, and by the 1890s those two erudite clergymen, S. Reynolds Hole, Dean of Rochester and author of the delightful *A Book about Roses*, and Andrew Foster-Melliar, Rector of Sproughton, Suffolk and author of *The Book of the Rose*, both devote many pages to advice on preparing roses for exhibition.

Dean Hole describes a visit to Nottingham to judge a working men's rose show. It was held in the upper room of a pub, the General Cathcart Inn, and the Dean was charmed by the high quality of the exhibits and by the blunt friendliness of the bricklayers, twist-hands, shoemakers, tailors and mechanics who had laboured with such love to produce them. One of the golden-hearted artisans told the Dean that throughout the winter he walked the mile from home to his allotment every morning before work, every evening after work, and often in his dinner hour as well. When one considers the length of a working day then compared to the usual 9 am to 5 pm of today, that is a real testimony to horticultural dedication. The same man, asked how he could afford the price of his new and expensive varieties of rose, replied 'by keping away from the beershops', which pleased the Dean who was not in favour of the working classes drinking.

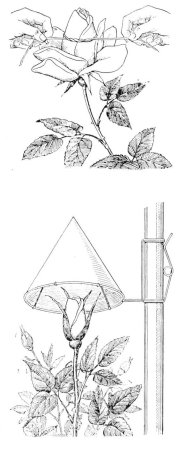

Preparing roses for exhibition.

In 1876 the National Rose Society had been formed, with Dean Hole as its first President, to bring under one umbrella amateur and professional growers and breeders, to set standards for the exhibiting of roses, and to provide a forum for the exchange of information about roses.

John Lindley wrote, 'It is in the flower that the beauty of plants chiefly resides,' and this idea has dominated the planning of English gardens up to the present day. Certainly from the mid-nineteenth century, for rose-lovers the emphasis was on the flower, not the plant as a whole, and on the flower for the show table or vase rather than the flower for the garden. The efforts of breeders were concentrated on producing larger, more perfect blooms in new colours, and rose lovers learned to look at each flower in close-up for its individual beauty, rather than at the wider scene of the rose garden as a whole.

Controversy developed as to whether rose gardens should be functional or ornamental. Foster-Melliar was firmly in the former camp, declaring that 'The idea is not the Rose for the Garden but the Garden for the Rose.' Dean Hole took the opposite view. He thought that a rose garden should not be '... the drill-ground of our Queen's bodyguard but the assemblage of her people – no formalism, no flatness, no monotonous repetition should prevail'.

One of the problems of the Victorian rose garden is that it must be extremely well done to succeed. For every garden that reaches the high standard we see today at Warwick Castle, Dean Hole and his contemporaries must have seen enough unsuccessful attempts at the formal style of rose garden to make them question the wisdom of attempting it.

Disillusion with formality in the rose garden was partly the result of a general movement away from formal gardening. In the eighteenth century, the imported French style of formal par-terres and avenues had been carried to such extremes of elab-oration that it could go no further and had to make way for the Landscape Movement. Similarly, in the nineteenth century, formal gardening on the smaller scale that prevailed in the sub-urban villa gardens of the emergent middle classes began to be seen as sterile and hostile to the plants that it was intended to display. People were ready to consider new ideas.

CHAPTER FIVE

The Cottage Garden Ideal

I know a little garden close,
Set thick with lily and red rose
Where I could wander if I might
From dewy morn till dewy night
And have one with me wandering.

William Morris *The Life and Death of Jason*

The inspiration needed to bring about a change from the exaggerated formality and artificiality in gardens at the turn of the century was to be found in the unassuming charm of modest, country cottage gardens, with their more natural style.

The leader of the new movement was William Robinson (1838–1935). Hot-tempered, opinionated and a fluent, persuasive writer, he was in many ways the ideal person to evangelise for Nature. Born in Ireland, he became garden boy to Sir Hunt Henry Johnson-Walsh and was foreman by the time he was twenty-one. After a row with his employer, he disappeared one night during the severe winter of 1861 having opened all the windows of the glasshouses. He made his way to London and was employed by Robert Marnock in the Royal Botanic Society's gardens in Regent's Park. One of his duties was the care of a collection of English wild flowers, and this led him to make frequent expeditions into the countryside, where he developed a passion for the landscape, and for the cottage gardens which harmonised so well with the landscape around them. Such a garden, 'Old Sally's', is described by Flora Thomson in *Lark Rise*: 'Wallflowers and tulips, lavender and sweet william, and pinks and old world roses with enchanting names – Seven Sisters, Maiden's Blush, moss rose, monthly rose, cabbage rose, blood rose . . . it seemed as though all the roses in Lark Rise had gathered together in that garden.'

Robinson's ideas were disseminated through his magazines *The Garden* and *Gardening Illustrated,* and his books, *The Wild Garden* (1870) and *The English Flower Garden* (1883). Indirectly he also reached a wide audience through the writing of Gertrude Jekyll who became a friend and whose own ideas were very much

'My Lady's Bower' by Theresa Sylvester Stannard (1898–1947).

in harmony with his. Robinson aspired to combine the simple pleasures of cottage gardens, where the decorative and the useful were artlessly fused, with an idealisation of nature. This movement towards more natural gardens did not occur in a vacuum: Bacon, Marnock and others had already made hints in this direction, and in some ways it is an interpretation of the ideal of the sublime landscape on a smaller, more domestic scale. Robinson's precursors include the Revd Henry Hill who wrote in *The Floracultural Cabinet and Florists' Magazine* in 1838 that the garden should appear to be more the offspring of nature and chance than of art and study.

Robinson, however, put his case with more force than most. He was not one to mince words. His writing was direct and sometimes brutal. He referred to Nathaniel Lloyd's book on topiary as 'The Poorest book that so far has disgraced the garden', and wrote that 'Clipping yews leads to leprous disfigurement, disease and death.' He disapproved of garden designers: 'In having these flowers we are happily free from the work of men who call themselves landscape architects, whose efforts are bad enough in gardens, but in the face of Nature, dreadful.' He also disapproved of feeding plants with manure: 'It occurred to me that the excreta of animals of various kinds spread under the windows of a house was not a good way.'

Contemporary designs for public landscapes as well as those for private gardens incurred Robinson's scorn. A new statue in one of London's parks provoked him into writing, 'large memorial confectionery groups ought not to be allowed to break up the space in the Parks. Lately, I am told, the fantastic idea of a playwright has been embodied in stone in Kensington Gardens. If each succeeding decade is to see outrages of that sort committed, what will eventually become of the repose and quiet grace of parks.' He is referring to the bronze (not stone) statue of J. M. Barrie's Peter Pan by the Serpentine in Hyde Park; several generations of children whose hands have worn away the bronze ears of its rabbits and the wings of its fairies must be grateful that Robinson's protest went unheeded.

His provocative style of writing forces attention, and his comments on the rose gardens of his day are as critical as Dean Hole's (the Dean was an admirer of Robinson's ideas). Robinson had this to say about the practice of treating roses as bedding plants:

'I give every rose a place to flower: never nearer than three feet. We never throw roses together like so many bedding annuals . . . and instead of bare beds I fill up between with the most beautiful flowers of the day: pansies, pinks, carnations.'

Although Robinson loved and was influenced by cottage gardens, he detested fake rusticity. He wrote, 'Few things about country houses and gardens are worse in effect than the so-called "rustic work". It is complex and ugly, its merit being that it rots away in a few years.'

Nevertheless, by advocating the cottage garden style, he was indirectly responsible for a great many pergolas, fences and other artefacts in rustic unpeeled larch, some of which produced an effect that was about as cottage-like in the gardens of grand houses like Polesden Lacey as the chef's version of shepherd's pie would be in their kitchens.

He disapproved of rose gardens set apart: 'Let us forever give up the stupid notion of growing our Roses only in a Rosery in some out of the way spot'; but not of rose gardens in general: 'The Rose must not come back in ugly ways, in Roses stuck and mostly starving on the tops of sticks, standards, or set in raw beds of manure and pruned hard and set thin so as to develop large blooms, but as the bloom is beautiful in all stages and sizes, Roses should be seen closely massed, feathering to the ground, the Queen of the flower garden in all ways . . . Roses must come back not only in beds, but in the old ways – over bower and trellis, and as bushes . . . so as to break up flat surfaces and give us light and shade where all is usually so level and hard.'

Dean Hole said the same sort of thing, but conjured up a more positive picture in this description of his ideal garden: 'Evergreen shrubs should screen and beautify by contrast the Roses blowing beneath . . . At irregular intervals [there are] Rose-clad mounds high enough to obstruct the view . . . to surprise, to vary and to conceal. On the level from which these mounds arose would be the beds and single specimens; at the corners my bowers and nooks. All the interior spaces not occupied with Roses should be turf.'

When Robinson had the opportunity to realise his ideas on the ground, he laid out rose gardens in a simple but conventional style. At Shrubland Park, for example, he replaced an elaborate pattern designed earlier by Sir Charles Barry with simply-shaped

OVERLEAF

Above left Cottage planting in a formal framework at West-well Manor, Oxfordshire.

Below left Roses spilling on to a stone terrace at Kiftsgate Court, Gloucestershire.

Right Lutyens' stone and timber pergola at Hestercombe, Somerset, where Gertrude Jekyll's planting has been restored.

beds set in lawns surrounded and divided by gravel walks. His innovation was to underplant the tea roses with red, pink and white carnations, and with snapdragons, evening primrose, lobelia, stocks, pansies, hyacinths and anemones. One group of roses shared their bed with zinnias. (I am not sure that that combination would have been an unqualified success.) In the walled garden at Uffington, near Stamford, he mixes plants boldly, including in beds of standard roses (which he says elsewhere he abominates) substantial groups of herbaceous plants: crimson peonies, verbascum, Japanese anemones.

The mixing of other plants with roses was, at the time, an important innovation, and is still a practice that is not adopted as often as it could be. It was advocated by both William Robinson and Gertrude Jekyll.

We are fortunate in being able not only to read Gertrude Jekyll's books but also to see with our own eyes what she was talking about in her down to earth yet eloquent fashion. The revival of interest in her ideas has led to the recreation of some of her planting schemes and we can examine and delight in them. For roses, Hestercombe in Somerset and Folly Farm in Berkshire are well worth visiting. Had it not been for the preservation of many of Miss Jekyll's planting plans, we would not have this advantage, for plants are the most fragile and ephemeral elements in the garden. The only legacy of her partnership with Sir Edwin Lutyens would have been his fine garden architecture. The clothing of the 'good bones' would have been a matter for speculation, based on the ideas expressed in Miss Jekyll's books.

Roses for English Gardens, published in 1902 in collaboration with Edward Mawley, is full of Gertrude Jekyll's creative ideas and good sense, as relevant today as they were then. On rose gardens she says, 'it is much to be desired that the formal and free ways should both be used.' She opens the reader's eyes to the possibilities of the humble briar rose and the Scottish roses, and teaches one to take advantage of their natural habit of growth, recommending Scotch Briars to 'fling themselves down from the tops of retaining walls, or to trail over banks', and climbers and ramblers to 'rush up a tree'.

Miss Jekyll's ideal English rose garden is 'embowered in native woodland', approached through dark yew, holly and Scotch fir. Situated in a small valley, the garden is long and narrow with

58

balustraded terraces and high retaining walls for roses to spill from. At the highest, wooded level, roses run up into the trees and there are scented brakes and tangles of Sweet briar. The rose beds are plain, long rectangles following the line of the valley at different levels and set off by the cool green of a lawn.

The Robinson-Jekyll garden philosophy of the marriage of the formal with the free has set the tone for gardening in the twentieth century. It is a philosophy that was espoused by the great partnership of Vita Sackville-West and Harold Nicolson and by their many followers among today's amateur and professional creators of beautiful gardens.

In spite of the contribution which old-fashioned roses were able to make towards achieving the Cottage Garden Ideal, the relentless fashion for Hybrid Tea and Floribunda roses which would keep on flowering all through the summer, sent many old roses out of commercial production and into, or close to, extinction. The steady decline in the popularity of old roses between the two World Wars, and the inevitable neglect of gardens and nurseries during the 'Digging for Victory' years of the Second World War, made the task of the loyal enthusiasts harder in the post-war years. Gardeners today have reason to be grateful to those like Edward Bunyard, Robert James, Graham Stuart Thomas and Vita Sackville-West for their work in searching out, preserving and propagating lost and rare varieties. And we have to thank, more than anyone, Graham Stuart Thomas for writing with such infectious enthusiasm about shrub roses in his books *The Old Shrub Roses*, *Climbing Roses Old and New*, and *Shrub Roses of Today*. These books have made old roses increasingly fashionable over the last thirty years, creating a demand that has encouraged nurserymen to produce an ever wider choice of shrub rose varieties. Through his books and by example at Mottisfont Abbey and in other National Trust gardens, Mr Thomas has influenced the design of rose gardens in a direction which would have pleased William Robinson and Gertrude Jekyll.

CHAPTER SIX

The New World

It is, I suppose, rather characteristic of an English colony that the gardens here are full of English plants and roses.

Letter from Charlotte Codley in New Zealand, 1850, quoted by Hazel le Rougetel in *A Heritage of Roses*

Just as Europe and Asia have their native rose species, so throughout North America the descendants of the thirty-two-million-year-old roses found fossilised in Colorado and Oregon are to be found thriving. Among the more ornamental species are that fine, robust shrub, *Rosa virginiana*, the dense, weed-smothering *R. nitida*, *R. nutkana*, *R. suffulta*, and *R. setigera*, the Prairie Rose.

These roses were, apparently, appreciated by the local population before the arrival of European settlers: Captain John Smith described thickets of wild roses planted by the Indians of James River to beautify their camps. The small number of native species was soon supplemented by roses brought from England by the Pilgrim Fathers and Edward Winslow, one of their number who landed in Massachusetts in 1620, reported the following year that 'an abundance of roses, white, red and damask, single but very sweet indeed,' had been planted by settlers.

Gradually more roses were imported. In 1699 William Penn, returning from a visit to England, brought eighteen rose bushes with him, and by 1773 Baron Henry von Stiegel's large collection of roses was famous. Perhaps there was friendly competition between the Baron and Lady Skipwith of Prestwold, Virginia, who modestly records in her gardening notebooks her own 'tolerable collection of Roses, amongst which are a double and single yellow, Marble and Cabbage.' At about the same time (1792 approximately), the roses in George Washington's garden at Mount Vernon were so prolific that 'Old Sall' took two days to pick them. Roses were a special interest at Mount Vernon. At least one hybrid raised there, a seedling from *R. setigera*, was of sufficiently high quality to go into commercial production: it was sold under the name 'Mary Washington'.

By this time roses were appearing regularly in nurserymen's lists. Prince of Flushing, Long Island listed in 1790 Moss Provence

Rosa virginiana 'Alba'.

(at three shillings the most expensive), Yellow, 'Rosa Mundi', Large Province, The Monthly, Red Damask, White Damask, Primrose, Musk, Cinnamon, Thornless, and 'American Wild, many sorts', these last a bargain at sixpence.

As might be expected, the areas of North America where rose-growing expanded most were those where a suitable climate coincided with a settled population. In many parts of the U.S.A. and Canada the climate is too extreme for roses to thrive, with burning sun in summer and fierce frosts in winter. Today this does not deter enthusiasts from providing the necessary protection to produce roses even in the most hostile environments. But in the early years it was in the colonised areas with relatively benign climates, such as Virginia and Pennsylvania, that rose-growing flourished. An interesting item of rose history can be seen near Boston where the eighteenth-century garden of John Quincy Adams contains a York Rose said to have been brought from England by Abigail Adams.

Charleston, Carolina is particularly important in the history of roses. It was there that John Champneys, a rice grower, first crossed 'Parson's Pink China' with the Musk rose, producing seedlings which, in their turn, gave rise to the first Noisette rose. Named after Philippe Noisette, a Charleston nurseryman and friend of Champneys, the significance of these roses was that they inherited the ability to flower continuously and were hardy. In 1817 Philippe Noisettte sent the first of these exciting new roses to his brother Louis in Paris and their use in breeding on both sides of the Atlantic has produced many long-term favourites, including 'Mme Alfred Carrière', 'Blush Noisette', 'Aimée Vibert' and 'Gloire de Dijon'.

The choice of rose varieties became ever wider, fed by the two-way transatlantic traffic of plant collectors and their prizes. Native American trees and shrubs were sent home by collectors like Peter Bartram throughout the eighteenth century to thrill European collectors and back came the latest rose hybrids, to enrich American breeding stock. By the 1920s the American Rose Society was able to list 445 American-bred roses, of which about 200 were then easily obtainable. Among them, popular survivors have been the Rugosa hybrids 'Sarah van Fleet' and 'Max Graf', the shrubs 'Little White Pet' and 'Bloomfield Abundance', ramblers 'American Pillar', 'Dorothy Perkins', 'Baltimore Belle' and

'May Queen', and climber 'Silver Moon'. As in Europe, such was the seductive allure of the new, that the old Alba, Gallica, Damask and Bourbon roses are conspicuous by their absence. By the 1930s, concern was being expressed about the loss from cultivation of the old-fashioned roses.

Mrs Keays, author of *Old Roses*, was one of the first enthusiasts to make a plea for the revival of old roses, pointing out their suitability for the gardens of period houses in Virginia and Connecticut. Fortunately two rosarians uninfluenced by fashion had maintained stocks of old roses throughout the 1920s: Lambertus Bobbink had imported 3,000 from France and Francis Lester had rescued as many as he was able from abandoned gold rush settlements in California.

Mrs Keays was instrumental in saving others. She describes the excitement of discovering the derelict rose garden of an abandoned country house high above Chesapeake Bay, with its simple, well-proportioned design of beds around a central lawn.

Reconstructions of period gardens can be seen at several historic houses, including the William Paca house at Annapolis, Maryland; the Moffatt-Ladd garden at Portsmouth, New Hampshire; the early nineteenth-century Adena Mansion at Chillicothe, Ohio; Old Westbury, Long Island, New York; Wyck, Germantown, Philadelphia; and at Mount Vernon and nearby Woodlawn Plantation. From the turn of the century onwards, such relatively modest gardens, which were domestic in their atmosphere and scale, began to be eclipsed by the increasingly extravagant and flamboyant displays created for the legendary industrial magnates. Many are open to visitors today.

The three-and-a-half acre rose garden at Hershey, Pennsylvania, originally created by Milton Hershey of chocolate fame, displays some 30,000 roses in terraced beds, with climbers and ramblers covering an impressive colonnade. The gardens have been expanded to cover twenty-three acres, and encompass a Chocolate Museum, Zoo America and the Hershey Museum of American Life. The Vanderbilt Mansion at Hyde Park, New York; the Biltmore Estate, Asheville, North Carolina (a 250-room French château); the Ringling Mansion at Sarasota, Florida, which is modelled on the Doge's Palace in Venice and the Hearst gardens at San Simeon, California, all boast spectacular and elaborate rose gardens.

In 1904, at about the same time that these gardens were being made, the world's first municipal rose garden was started at Elizabeth Park, Hartford, Connecticut. Rose trials have been held there since 1910. The original garden, laid out around a rustic summer house typical of the period, displays a collection of Hybrid Perpetual roses dating from 1903, some of which are very rare today, with early climbers and ramblers on arches around the perimeter. Altogether there are 15,000 roses representing 1,000 varieties. The roses are displayed in many different ways, including pillar roses supported on seven-foot Sitka spruce poles with short lateral branches. The high standard set at Elizabeth Park is mirrored in municipal rose gardens in every North American city of any size, even in the most unpromising climates, and some feature model backyard gardens and horticultural advice centres.

America's biggest rose garden is, as might be expected, in Texas, in the centre of the U.S.A.'s biggest commercial rose-growing area. The Municipal Rose Garden at Tyler covers twenty-two acres, formally landscaped against a wooded background. There are pools, fountains and gazebos, and the 38,000 roses provide colour from May, when they are at their best, until October. There is a fine sunken garden enclosed by high walls, terraces of miniature roses in raised beds and every kind of arch, pillar and pergola.

In the southern hemisphere, where there are no native rose species, roses and rose gardens have been established by colonists and expatriates yearning not only for the green, green grass but also for the red, red roses of home, so that today there are Rose Societies in Argentina, Australia, Bermuda, New Zealand, South Africa and Uruguay. In all these countries, the design of rose gardens tends to be caught in a nostalgic time-warp, symmetrical beds of Hybrid Tea and Floribunda roses being cut out of lawns which need copious watering twice daily to achieve the Home Counties rectory greensward to which they aspire.

In Australia, in Melbourne in the state of Victoria, one of the earliest of antipodean rose gardens provides the site for one of the most recent and most spectacular. The earlier rose garden at Werribee Park was laid out in 1877 by two Scottish brothers, Thomas and Andrew Chirnside, when they built a sixty-room Italianate mansion on their 1,000-acre estate. When the Rose

Above left Climbing roses on George Washington's pergola at Mount Vernon.

Above right Immaculate topiary in the Rose Garden at Woodland Park, Seattle.

Below The International Rose Test Garden at Portland.

Society of Victoria was started in 1901, Andrew's son, George Chirnside, was one of its first patrons, so it is appropriate that the new State Rose Garden, proposed in the 1970s and implemented in the 1980s, should be made at Werribee. Designed by J. L. Priestly of the National Rose Society of Australia, the ambitious project occupies twelve acres of the estate and is laid out in the shape of a vast, stylised Tudor Rose. There are Hybrid Teas, Floribundas, standards, weeping standards, climbers and ramblers, in beds, on pillars, trellises, tripods, arches, festoons and pergolas. The fact that some 6,000 rose plants were donated by Rose Society members is evidence of the healthy state of rose gardens throughout Australia.

The most striking new ideas contributed by the New World have been concerned with large-scale landscape planting. In the U. S. A., as early as the 1920s, Charles Downing Lay, editor of *Landscape Architecture*, advocated the use of wild roses, either in masses of one variety or mixed. Their hips would provide winter interest and their bare branches would be 'full of delicate, misty colours when seen in mass . . . from pale green to rusty greens, bronzy reds and quiet crimson.' He suggested that, used along meadow streams, on rocky hillsides or on sandy beaches, they would give the appearance of natural wilderness, provide good cover for birds and be 'impassable for man or boy'. He recommends *R. lucida* to prevent coastal erosion and *R. carolina* to plant in damp meadows.

In *The Rose in America* (1923) McFarland describes a road, leading out of Los Angeles, lined with roses on both sides for twenty miles, and several miles of railway cutting covered in 'Dorothy Perkins' to improve the view from the train and to prevent erosion. *R. rugosa* seems to be the only rose used extensively in Europe for the landscaping purposes that Charles Downing Lay had in mind. Valued for its dense, healthy foliage which colours well in autumn, and for its fine display of hips, it has become ubiquitous in shopping precincts, at highway roundabouts and in motorway central reservations, and we may get tired of it before long. There are other robust and disease-free roses that could be chosen to introduce greater variety, and there is scope for their imaginative use to make the landscape one big rose garden.

PART TWO

---❦---

The Design of Rose Gardens

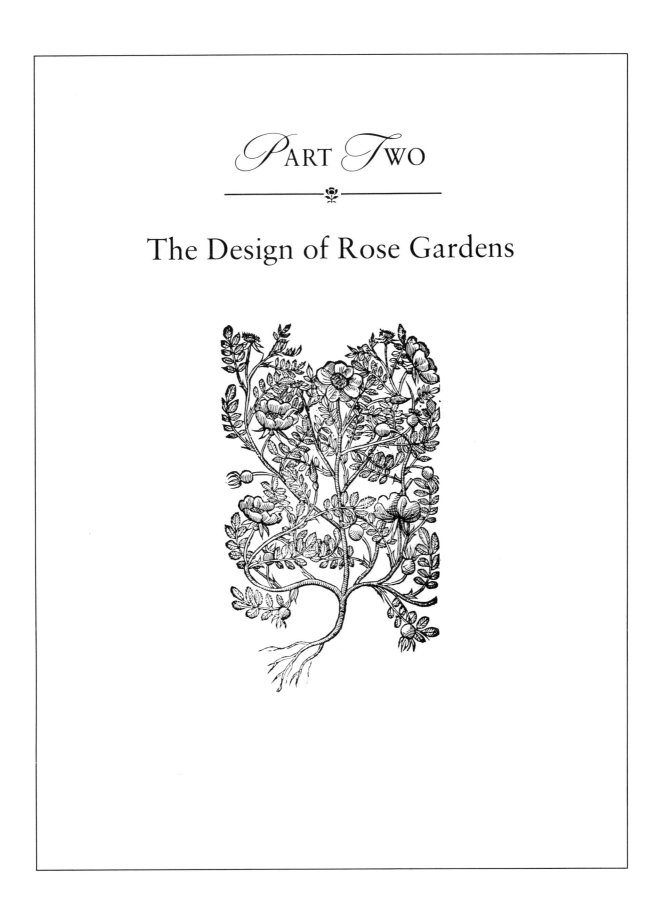

❦ CHAPTER SEVEN

The Versatile Rose

What a diversity and yet what a harmony of colour! There are white Roses, Striped Roses, Blush roses, Pink Roses, Rose Roses, Carmine Roses, Crimson Roses, Scarlet Roses, Vermilion Roses, Maroon Roses, Purple Roses, Roses almost Black, and Roses of a glowing Gold. What a diversity, and yet what a harmony of outline! Dwarf Roses and Climbing Roses closely carpeting the ground, Roses that droop in snowy foam like fountains, and Roses that stretch out their branches upwards as though they would kiss the sun.

Dean Hole *A Book About Roses* (1874)

Roses can perform in so many different ways, and yet gardens where the wonderful diversity described by Dean Hole is fully utilised are few and far between. They are the exception to a rule which seems to dictate that (to misquote Gertrude Stein), 'A rose is a rose is a rose and if it's not a Hybrid Tea, it must be a Floribunda.'

But 'A rose is a rose is . . .' also a Damask, a Gallica, a Bourbon, an Alba, a Hybrid Perpetual, a Polyantha, a Noisette, a Climber and a Rambler.

The extraordinary variety of colour, size and shape of plant and flower in the *genus rosa* can be confusing, but the different types of rose and their ancestry and progeny are lucidly explained in Graham Stuart Thomas's books which cannot fail to enlarge the knowledge of readers already converted to old roses and to make converts of those who still have the pleasure of discovery to come.

Mr Thomas also gives detailed and accurate descriptions of individual rose varieties and does not forget the importance of scent, foliage and habit of growth. Other good sources of information are the catalogues of rose nurseries, especially those of Peter Beales and David Austin (both have very comprehensive lists and specialise in old roses), and Roses du Temps Passé, whose smaller list is selective and carefully chosen.

With so much information available, there is no need for a comprehensive list of roses here, but you will find in Appendix B short, selective lists of roses with notes on their suitability for

Rosa filipes 'Kiftsgate' at Longstock Water Gardens, Hampshire.

different situations. When considered as flowering shrubs for various uses in the garden, it soon becomes clear that important qualities are sometimes neglected, such as the shape of the plants, the colour and texture of their foliage, and their autumn and winter display of fruit.

In all garden design the shape and texture of the plants is at least as important as the colour and shape of the flowers. The rose provides, in its flowers, glorious colour and scent for a few months of the year. Its other qualities as a flowering shrub were less important in the days when the rose garden was a separate part of a larger whole, to be visited in June and July and ignored for the other ten months of the year, except by a team of gardeners whose duties included feeding, weeding, spraying, pruning and training the roses.

But things are usually different now. Space is at a premium and rose gardens must earn their keep for a longer season. This can be achieved in two ways. The way that has been generally accepted for the past fifty years or so is to stick to the traditional patterns of symmetrical beds cut out of the the lawn, but to plant in those beds the Floribunda and Hybrid Tea roses which modern growers have bred for continuity of flower. The choice ranges from single to fully double flowers, in clusters or as single blooms, in every hue of the spectrum except blue and green. In massed plantings they can be truly spectacular, as can be seen by visiting the Royal National Rose Society's Gardens of the Rose near St Albans, or the City of Aberdeen where every route into the city is lined with roses. But in most private gardens planting for massed colour effects is neither practical nor appropriate, and the effect that is usually seen is one of spots of different, unco-ordinated colours on plants of randomly mixed height and vigour, with a background of sparse, coarse foliage above bare soil or the untidy heaps of animal excreta that William Robinson deplored.

In making such a garden, the gardener is choosing to ignore the whole range of old roses whose beauty, though fleeting, has a delicacy not found in most modern roses, whose scent is unrivalled and whose form and foliage is often pleasing. More-over, a rose garden without old roses would be a poor illustration of the poetry of the rose. That many of them also require little or no pruning is an extra bonus.

There are, of course, exceptions to the rule that Floribunda and Hybrid Tea roses make stiff, ungainly bushes. Some will, if pruned only lightly, and planted close in groups of three or five, form reasonably dense and shapely shrubs. They include, among Floribundas, 'Apricot Nectar', 'Escapade', 'Yesterday', 'Eye Paint', 'Chanelle', 'Pink Parfait' and 'Iceberg'; and among Hybrid Teas, 'Frau Karl Druschki', 'Just Joey', 'Pink Favourite', 'Pascali', 'Lady Sylvia', 'Ophelia', 'Westfield Star' and 'Mrs Oakley Fisher'. Many of those described in catalogues as having 'compact' or 'bushy' growth are also suitable for use in this way.

Good foliage is a great asset on any plant, as a background to its own flowers, as a background to other plants, or simply to provide colour and texture which harmonise or contrast with other plants nearby. There are several roses which are worth growing for their foliage alone, the flowers being a pretty bonus. First among them is *Rosa glauca* (formerly called *R. rubrifolia*). Its leaves are a unique pinky-purplish blue-grey on a shrub which puts out long arching shoots reaching a height and spread of about 6ft × 5ft/2m × 1.5m. The small, bright pink, single flowers look pretty against the leaves, but are soon over, to be followed by a good crop of dark red hips. It makes a fine background to other roses, and is useful to link grey-leaved shrubs to those with purple foliage such as *Cotinus coggyria* 'Foliis Purpureis', purple-leaved hazel, beech or prunus. It is also a good foil to roses with purple and blue-pink flowers.

Several roses have scented foliage and two species are outstanding in this respect: one plant of either will fill a garden with their perfume after rain. One is *R. primula*, known as the Incense Rose and raised from seed collected near Samarkand, an irresistibly romantic origin and, as if that were not enough, it is a very pretty shrub with arching branches of delicate ferny leaves, smothered in late spring with equally delicate single primrose-yellow flowers. In Britain it is the earliest rose to flower and has the style of a spring, rather than a summer shrub. Where there is space to allow it freedom of growth, it makes a graceful shrub some 6ft × 8ft/2m × 2.5m, but in smaller gardens can be clipped to form a hedge or smaller bush. To enjoy its scent, plant it where you will pass it often, perhaps between garage and back door.

The other rose with fragrant leaves which I would not be without, for its scent, its fleeting charm in flower, its cheerful red

Left Hips and foliage of *Rosa rugosa.*

Right Hips of *Rosa moyesii* 'Sealing Wax' with *Achillea filipendula* 'Gold Plate'.

hips and its romantic associations, is *Rosa rubiginosa,* or *R. eglanteria*: the Eglantine or Sweetbriar of Chaucer, Spenser, and Shakespeare. A native of Northern Europe including Britain, this must have been one of the first roses to be brought from the wild into the garden. It was the rose used on trellises, fences and arbours in the earliest gardens, or clipped to form an impenetrable hedge. It was one of Francis Bacon's favourite plants, and he recommended it as 'Very delightful to set under a parlour or lower chamber window'; Canon Ellacombe in his book *In a Gloucestershire Garden* describes it trained to cover the walls of a two-storied house at Tintern; and the front garden of Mrs Copperfield's house in Charles Dickens' *David Copperfield* was separated from the road by a sweetbriar hedge. Hybrids from *R. rubiginosa* which have inherited its scented foliage include 'Mannings Blush', a compact shrub growing to about 5ft/1.5m, with neat bright green leaves and small clusters of double, blush-white flowers. It makes a good hedge, clipped or unclipped, and is a dense, shapely shrub to use in front of taller roses of more open and lax habit. Smaller (4ft × 3ft/1.2m × 1m), and compact with small, crimson double flowers, is 'La Belle Distinguée', and both 'Lord Penzance' and 'Lady Penzance' are good, he with buff flowers, she with coppery-salmon, both with bright red hips.

Scottish, Burnet, *spinosissima* and *pimpinellifolia* are, con-

Above left The Noisette rose 'Rêve d'Or'.

Above right *Rosa gallica* 'Versicolor' (Rosa Mundi).

Below left The modern shrub rose 'Constance Spry'.

Below right The rambler 'Wedding Day'.

fusingly, all names for the same class of roses. Like the sweet-briars, they have dense, tidy foliage and delicate, fairly small flowers, but are smaller (up to 4ft/1.2m) and sometimes prostrate. They are also very prickly, hardy and tough, happy in poor soils where few other roses would survive, therefore excellent for a rose garden in unpromising conditions. Indeed, using Burnet roses you could make a rose garden on a stony bank or on a sand dune. They will drape themselves nicely over a retaining wall if planted on the top, making a change from the tired cliché of aubretia and alyssum. Among the best are the Dunwich Rose, 'Falkland' with greyish leaves and very pale lilac-pink flowers, 'Double White', 'Mary Queen of Scots' and 'Stanwell Perpetual' (true to its name, it flowers in Britain from May till Christmas).

It is sad that beauty of foliage and grace of form have, to a great extent, been bred out of roses in favour of size, shape and colour of flower. But fortunately species roses are now more widely available to delight us with these qualities. Besides those already mentioned, they vary from the prostrate *R. nitida*, 2ft/0.6m high and spreading by suckers, or *R. paulii*, forming dense ground cover over an area up to 12ft/3.6m in diameter, to giants 10ft/3m tall, like *R. macrophylla* and *R. moyesii*. *R. hugonis* and its hybrids bear artlessly charming little single flowers with Granny-Smith-green foliage early in the season. In flower they are like great arching bushes covered in primroses, and after flowering their fresh green makes a good background to later roses of all colours, and a good host for clematis. They look good, too, as specimens in orchard or meadow.

Those species which bear greyish leaves are valuable in mixed plantings: of these, *R. fedtschenkoana*, *R. murielae* and *R. willmottiae* have beautiful, arching young shoots, grey with a white-ish bloom and pink thorns, which gives an elegant effect. They are best planted where one can see the whole plant.

Alba roses have good, healthy foliage, usually described as grey-green. The leaves are a fairly pale green, overlaid with a faint blue-ish-white bloom, as if they had been dipped in milk. *Rosa alba semi-plena*, 'Maiden's Blush' (or, with French sophistication, 'Cuisse de Nymphe'), 'Celestial' and 'Queen of Denmark' are beautiful shrubs and have everything except a long flowering season: they are strong, tidy and disease-free, with exquisitely delicate, sweetly scented flowers, and they will grow in light shade. Growing to 5–6ft/1.5–1.8m, they make a quiet but fresh-looking background to shorter, later roses such as 'The Fairy' or 'Yesterday' or, in a stronger colour scheme, reds and purples such as 'Rosemary Rose' (its reddish-purple young foliage is a bonus) or 'Cardinal Hume'.

Autumn colour of leaf and fruit has, like delicacy of foliage and grace of habit, been bred out of most hybrid roses, so that it is again to the Species that we must look. A rose garden designed to reach its climax in the autumn would be planted mainly with Species and their near hybrids. It need not be dull at other seasons, since many of the roses with the finest display of hips are also handsome in flower. Such a garden would be informal in character. The ideal site would be an old orchard or a paddock bounded by a hedgerow where some of the more rampant climbers could grapple their way upwards and sideways to hang their bunches of hips in cascades: *R. helenae* is ideal, with dark foliage and dense clusters of creamy-white flowers in early summer which give way in autumn to prolific small red hips showing up well at a distance. It can be followed in flower by *R. moschata* 'Flori-bunda', the Musk Rose of the poets, with its powerfully scented white flowers and small, oval, orange hips. It has the additional advantage of fresh-looking light green leaves which look good clambering over heavy foliage such as yew, holly or *Prunus pissardii*.

Hybrid ramblers which give a good display of hips include 'Kew Rambler', bearing large clusters of soft pink scented flowers late in the season, and small, orange hips. Plentiful, small, greyish leaves give added value and, if space allowed, I would plant at its feet its parent *R. soulieana*, a shrub reaching 10ft/3m square, from which the grey colouring and orange hips are inherited. 'Rambling Rector' is also tough and reliable up a tree, over a hedge, or over an ugly shed or any other eyesore. It smothers itself in flowers (cream fading to white) and gives a good display of small, oval hips.

R. filipes 'Kiftsgate' and its near relation 'Treasure Trove' are often recommended for growing into trees, but be warned that they must have a worthy host: the original plant at Kiftsgate Court in Gloucestershire is 100ft/30m wide, reaches the top of a mature copper beech and is still spreading. It is a slow starter, but once it gets going there is no stopping it, and it could completely destroy a small garden. It is a great spectacle in flower and in fruit, and has the advantage of leaves which are coppery when young and turn to russet in the autumn. In a garden which has the misfortune to be guarded by a row of Leyland cypress I would plant 'Kiftsgate' at the feet of these threatening soldiers in their drab greatcoats and let it do its worst.

If this proposed autumn rose garden were not already enclosed, I would make an informal hedge around it of roses chosen for their fruit or autumn leaves, interspersed with sober evergreens to set them off: privet, *Elaeagnus × ebbingei* and *Viburnum rhytidophyllum* for quick effect; hollies, *Choisya ternata*, *Osmanthus burkwoodii* and *Viburnum tinus* (these last three give the bonus of flowers before the roses) for the more patient gardener. I would give priority to roses which do double duty in the autumn, providing changing leaf colour as well as hips, so the Rugosas, with their bright golden-yellow leaves and hips like small tomatoes would be my first choice. Their robust, dense, disease-free growth and hardiness makes them particularly good for hedging and many varieties bear flowers and fruit with great generosity. 'Scabrosa' (an unappealing name for a splendid plant) has huge, orange-red hips and very large single flowers coloured a rich magenta crimson, a good companion in a lush colour scheme for 'Roseraie de l'Haÿ', which has semi-double crimson-purple flowers and very good autumn leaves, but, alas, seldom produces hips. The colour of these roses might seem too harshly opulent if it were not relieved by their cream-coloured stamens. They should be separated from flowers of more delicate colouring by the white flowers of the single *R. rugosa* 'Alba' whose large orange-red hips appear with the late flowers. 'Nyveldt's White' is similar but a smaller, more compact shrub. Two double white Rugosas, useful to contrast with the singles, are 'Blanc Double de Coubert' and 'Schneezwerg' ('Snow Dwarf'), with pretty, smaller flowers and small orange-red hips. Perhaps the best of all Rugosas, either in a mixed planting or as a hedge on its own, is 'Frau Dagmar Hartopp' (or 'Hastrup'), with large silver-pink single flowers, crimson hips and good autumn colour.

Many of the Species roses which fruit spectacularly are best planted as single specimens so that the graceful arching of branches weighed down with hips can be appreciated. If I had space for only half a dozen I would choose *R. moyesii* 'Geranium', less

The new English shrub rose 'Graham Thomas'.

gaunt than the species, with the same large, red, flagon-shaped hips; *R. farreri* 'Persetosa' (the Threepenny Bit Rose), wider than its height of 5 or 6ft/1.6 or 1.8m, with tiny, ferny leaves which turn purple and crimson and lots of little orange hips; 'Master Hugh' for its profuse, large, single, bright pink flowers and very large flagon-shaped hips; *R. woodsii fendleri* with deep red pendulous hips; *R. villosa*, or *R. pomifera* (apple-bearing), or its hybrid 'Wolley-Dod' (named after yet another Reverend rosarian) with huge, dark crimson hips; and *R. forrestiana*, its strong, arching branches strung with bright red, bottle-shaped hips.

At the feet of these, low ground-cover roses could sprawl: *R. nitida* with scarlet and crimson leaves and red hips, the Burnet roses 'Falkland' and 'Mary Queen of Scots' with blackish-maroon hips, and the lovely Dunwich Rose. Where there are areas of rough ground or banks to be covered, crawling roses with near-evergreen foliage can be used to contrast with the yellow leaves of the Rugosas or the red leaves of *R. nitida* and *R. virginiana*. Those that are genuinely weed-smothering, provided they are planted in clean ground to start with, include the species *R. wichuraiana* with small, glossy dark leaves and clusters of small white single flowers which, usefully, bloom when most other roses have finished. The shoots root down as they travel, so that it can cover a wide area or can be stopped as necessary. 'Max Graf' behaves in the same way, and the strong floriferous 'Wedding Day' and 'Albéric Barbier' will also make dense ground cover. 'Félicité et Perpétue' will make a dense, wide mound smothered in little white rosettes bursting from crimson-striped buds; it is tough as can be and will tolerate shade. There are many more Species and hybrid shrub roses that make good ground cover, including the new, tidy prostrate varieties such as 'White Bells', 'Pink Bells' and 'Grouse' and its relations.

Most of the roses I have described are well suited to the wilder, more natural parts of the garden, thriving without much effort on the part of the gardener, and providing cover and food for wild life. The aim in a wild garden is to create an idealised landscape on a small scale, where both native and exotic plants can thrive in an ecologically balanced environment. Birds, insects and aquatic animals are encouraged in these modern Edens and, to a lesser extent, animals, although there are not many gardeners who would wish to make habitats for rabbits, mice, moles and

A formal garden plan from William Lawson's *New Orchard and Garden* (1618) includes topiary figures (A), espaliers (A), orchard (B), knot (C) and symmetrical vegetable plots (D).

foxes. Such evocations of a paradise lost in the twentieth century to concrete and tarmac indicate that the art of gardening, which has been somewhat aimlessly pursued in recent decades, has again developed a philosophical purpose. Garden history has completed a circle, and we are again striving, as the earliest gardeners did, to shut out the hostile world by enclosing our own plots securely.

At the opposite pole of gardening fashion is the revival of formality in the garden. Twenty years ago there was hardly a straight line or a geometric curve to be seen: shrub beds, lawns and even swimming pools were shaped like kidneys and amoebae, and paths twisted as tortuously as intestines. But now, pleasure is again derived from geometric shapes, from vistas centred on a viewpoint within the house, and from axes and cross-axes. The satisfaction of the immemorial symmetry of circle and square is rediscovered and delight is found in intricate patterns. Not since the seventeenth century can so many knots have been tied in box, lavender and santolina. This desire for orderly arrangement is a reaction against the disorder outside the garden walls.

The rose can rise to the occasion. Climbing roses to form the vertical framework of the formal garden and to clothe the arches and arbours at its focal points are legion; there are shrubs of all sizes and colours to soften the outlines of rectilinear beds and neat little roses such as 'Little White Pet', 'Yesterday', and 'The Fairy' to fill the interstices of knots. Charming low hedges and edgings can be made with 'Hermosa', 'Nathalie Nypels', 'Old Blush China', 'Rose de Meaux' or 'Pompon de Bourgogne'. In the formal garden the nurseryman's skill in grafting roses on to single stems is revived to make weeping fountains of 'Crimson Showers', 'Débutante', 'Goldfinch', 'Albéric Barbier' or 'Nozomi', and mop-headed mini trees of 'Ballerina', 'Rosa Mundi', 'Empress Josephine' and many more.

There is a rose for every situation in the garden, formal or informal, and for most situations a dozen or more to choose from. The gardener is spoilt for choice.

CHAPTER EIGHT

The Genius of the Place

Our England is a garden that is full of stately views,
Of borders, beds and shrubberies and lawns and avenues,
With statues on the terraces and peacocks strutting by,
But the Glory of the Garden lies in more than meets the eye.

Rudyard Kipling, *The Glory of the Garden*

A garden does not exist in a vacuum and, whether a rose garden is being planned from scratch or made by adapting an existing garden, it should be considered in relation to its surroundings.

The site will influence the layout and the planting in a number of practical ways. Is the area large or small? Its size will dictate the scale of the planting to a great extent. The small back yard of a town house will be overwhelmed by half a dozen large shrubs, whilst a large, open expanse of ground will render small, delicate plants insignificant. Is the site long and narrow, broadly rectangular, or awkwardly irregular? Will it be better to emphasise the shape or to disguise it? Is the site flat, or does it slope towards the house, away from it or at an oblique angle to it? Should you take advantage of the slope to create different levels? This may mean going to the expense of hiring a digging machine and building retaining walls and flights of steps. Perhaps it would be better to accept the natural lie of the land, planning the planting either to enhance it or disguise it.

What is the aspect? If it faces north or east, is shade the only problem, or is it also exposed to harsh winter winds? If it faces south or west, is it exposed to dessicating summer winds and de-stabilising spring and autumn gales? Is it in a frost pocket? Is the soil free-draining or moisture-retentive? Acid or alkaline? Careful analysis of all these factors, erring on the pessimistic side, will help you to make difficult decisions about the garden and will save you from making expensive mistakes. Even if conditions seem really unpromising, there is no need to despair. There are roses, and other plants to grow among them, that will do well in the most inhospitable of soils and in the harshest of climates. The secret of success is to make the most of what is possible and

A rose border at Elsing Hall, Norfolk.

not to attempt the impossible, except, perhaps, as a deliberate experiment.

Such practical factors will narrow the options. But there are also aesthetic questions to be considered, and the answers to them will be more subjective.

Whether the rose garden is adjacent to the house or in another part of the garden, the architecture of the house and any out-buildings are important. The garden may either echo the style of the house or contrast with it. An ugly house can be improved by planting climbing plants against its walls and planning the garden so that the eye is always drawn away from the house into the garden or towards a distant view. On the other hand, if the house is handsome, the plan can focus on it, and the planting will be planned to complement the architecture. It is not necessarily right to make a formal, symmetrical garden for a classical house and a rambling, cottage-style garden for a 'romantic' house. It is sometimes preferable to soften the severity of a classical building with luxuriant informality in the garden, or to unite the disparate elements of a rambling house by setting it in the framework of a formal garden. But these are decisions that should be taken deliberately and not left to chance.

It is useful to consider the inside of the house as well as the outside. It will reflect the personalities of the owners and the garden should do the same. If you are designing your own rose garden, think about how you have arranged the rooms in your house. Are they formal and elegant? Tidy, with a place for every-thing and everything in its place? Or is there a clutter of furniture and objects, with tangled knitting jostling for space with children's toys and dog's bone? If the latter, and you have a vision of a French-style rose garden with couture ramblers neatly trained to their supports and immaculately tailored topiary, forget your vision and settle for 'a sweet disorder in the dress' *à l'anglaise*. Look, too, at the colour schemes and patterns in the house. If the curtains are covered in apricot-coloured roses, it would be better not to plant magenta roses immediately outside the window.

The garden is at the threshold of the house; it also stands between the house and the landscape beyond. Looking, as it does, both ways, the garden can link the house to the world outside. However, there may be good reasons for making the garden turn

82

its back on the house – the landscape may be of such beauty that it exerts a strong pull – or for making it embrace the house in order to protect it from a landscape of gasometers or motorway lanes. Heeding Pope's advice to 'Consult the Genius of the Place', you may reveal an Evil Genius, in which case the garden must turn in on itself and create its own private world, becoming an oasis in a desert of concrete.

Rose gardens are often made in close proximity to the house, on or immediately below a formal terrace, or carved out of a lawn or within a walled or hedged enclosure (sometimes in a redundant kitchen garden). They can occupy the whole back yard of a terraced town house or the whole front garden of a semi-detached house in the suburbs. All these situations suggest a measure of formality and a respect for the architecture of the house when choosing the materials and style of walls, paving, steps and other built elements, though the planting may be irregular and luxuriant in counterpoint to the rectilinear layout.

There are not many rose gardens made just at the point where the garden meets the wider landscape and yet roses are ideal for such a situation. A garden on the lines of the rose garden for autumn described in Chapter 7 could blend into a rural landscape, with garden roses, honeysuckles and foxgloves reaching out to their native sisters in the hedgerows. In my own Cotswold country I would make narrow paths between banks of shrub roses wreathed in clematis, to echo the dog roses and old man's beard that sprawl over the local limestone escarpment, mercifully masking the raw cuttings of new motorways and bypasses. There are roses to suit every aspect of England's richly diverse landscape: even windswept sand dunes are blithely colonised by the Burnet roses.

The majority of gardens, of course, are not surrounded by beautiful rural landscapes and, sadly, in the twentieth century, most urban landscapes leave much to be desired and are not on a sufficiently human scale to inspire gardens which relate to them. But there are situations in unspoilt villages and in rare city pockets untouched by new development, where gardens form part of an integrated scene that should be respected. Self-consciously pretty villages, where the road verges are cut like bowling greens and the houses sport 'ye olde' mullion windows outside and reproduction horse brasses inside, dictate their own style of gardening,

OVERLEAF

Left Formal rose beds and hedge make a firm boundary between the architecture of the verandah and the distant view.

Right:

Above Rambler roses on an iron pergola frame the wooden bridge in Claude Monet's garden at Giverny, France.

Below left Roses framing an unselfconscious cottage door at Stanway in the Cotswolds, with *Anemone Hybrida* and bergenia at their feet.

Below right An inviting, arched doorway of silvery weathered timber framed with *Hydrangea petiolaris* at Barrington Court, Somerset.

often as determinedly quaint as a pantomime stage set for *Mother Goose* or *Jack and the Beanstalk*. But there are also working agricultural villages, and houses in them, where old-fashioned cottage gardens are entirely appropriate today, just as they were in earlier days, and roses round the door and amongst the cabbages provide the continuity of an honest tradition.

One should never be ashamed to borrow styles and ideas from the past. Even the ideas which seem newest to us are often rooted in the past. They have evolved from a vast reservoir filled by centuries of creativity and constantly replenished. The more familiar one can become with the contents of that source of riches – by reading, by looking at pictures and, above all, by visiting gardens – the better the prospect of making a garden that is special. But ideas should not be transplanted willy-nilly. They need to be digested and adapted, so that they appear to develop from the site, rather than being imposed on it.

There is one more quality which should be considered. It is abstract, elusive, and difficult to describe, yet there are some very beautiful gardens which cannot be called wholly successful, because they lack it. It is the element in a garden which stirs the emotions and can, perhaps, best be described as 'mood'. There is an infinity of different moods, melancholy, tranquil, sober, frivolous, opulent, or guileless. A garden's mood may simply be part of the Genius of the Place or else it is invoked by the ghosts of gardens and gardeners past. It is difficult to deliberately create a mood, but it is only too easy to destroy one.

The mood of a garden is felt more through the plants than through the structures that frame them. Of all plants, there is none so capable of distilling a wide variety of different moods than the rose. The child-like simplicity of 'Cécile Brunner', 'Perle d'Or' or 'Paquerette' (Gertrude Jekyll thought the latter, now no longer in cultivation, the perfect plant for a child's grave); the cool elegance of 'Virgo'; the sumptuous luxury of 'Guinée' or 'Constance Spry'; the bar-maid tartiness of 'Super Star': all have their contribution to make in creating different moods. If I have fallen into the trap of endowing roses with human, feminine characteristics, that is because they do seem indisputably feminine. One might catch oneself referring to a snowdrop as a brave little fellow or a pansy as a cheeky chap, but a rose is always 'she'. Many rose-lovers refer to them thus, regardless of their

86

names, just as, to a sailor, a ship is always 'she'. It sounds a little strange to hear Cardinals de Richelieu and Hume, Captains Ingram, Christy and Hayward, three Dukes, five Generals, and the stalwart Parkdirektor Riggers all thus emasculated.

CHAPTER NINE

Planning a Rose Garden

Our England is a garden, and such gardens are not made
By singing:- 'Oh, how beautiful,' and sitting in the shade.

Rudyard Kipling, *The Glory of the Garden*

Whether the rose garden is to be large or small, formal or informal, flat or terraced, there are certain general principles regarding the various components that make up the whole, which are worth considering before a plan is made. The plan can be made on paper, after accurate measurement of the site, including any changes of level, or directly on to the ground, using pegs and strong twine to mark straight lines and rope or hosepipe to delineate curves.

One of the most important components will be the boundary which forms the background to the plants. The bleak and inconsequential appearance of a pattern of beds cut out of a large expanse of lawn has already been commented on, and the enclosure of the rose garden by walls, fences or hedges will solve that problem, providing a feeling of security and intimacy within and adding an element of surprise on entering.

The site may already be enclosed or partly enclosed by house walls or garden walls. If so, the colour and materials of the walls will influence the colour scheme of the roses and any other plants grown among them. Most pink roses have a blue tone to them, and do not show to advantage against the orange tone of most bricks, which are kinder to roses in the white, yellow and apricot-orange colour range. If blue pinks and purple reds are an essential part of the colour scheme, a harmonious background can be provided by disguising brickwork with a dense, close-hugging climber chosen for its foliage: ivy, *Euonymus fortunei* 'Coloratus' with dark green leaves which turn crimson-purple in the autumn and winter or, for a really large expanse of wall, one of the Parthenocissus varieties. Climbing roses can be trained against the green background thus provided, an effect which can be seen brilliantly executed against ivy-clad walls ten feet high at Alderley Grange in Gloucestershire. A sober background to the roses could equally well be provided by one of the climbing plants that will

88

The parterre at Blickling Hall, Norfolk.

flower before the roses (*Clematis alpina*, *C. armandii*, *C. calycina*, *C. cirrhosa*, *C. macropetala*, wisteria, *Lonicera periclymenum* 'Belgica') or, when the once-flowering roses are past their best, *Clematis campaniflora*, *C. orientalis*, *C. tangutica*, *C. viticella*, *C.* 'Ernest Markham', *C.* 'Gipsy Queen', *C.* 'Lady Betty Balfour', *C.* 'Ville de Lyon', passiflora, trachelospermum and solanum.

If walls are to be built from scratch, the architecture of the house should be respected, and local materials and methods used if possible. If the real thing is too expensive, a wall of breezeblocks rendered and painted in a suitable neutral shade can soon be hidden by climbing plants. A sturdy timber fence of vertical boarding and posts bedded in concrete is another less expensive alternative and will last for up to ten years if treated regularly with preservative (but not creosote which can damage plants).

The poor man's wall is a hedge and, where a dark, solid background is needed, a hedge may be the most appropriate boundary. If well looked after, it will last as long as a wall but. requires more attention. Quick-growing hedging plants such as Leyland cypress, lonicera or privet with their promise of an almost instant effect, offer a temptation that should be resisted at all costs. Their quick growth is partly due to their wide-ranging roots which are so efficient in their quest for water and nutrients that they will rob any other plant within yards of them. Lonicera and privet put out new shoots so rapidly that a trim every few weeks is needed during the summer months to keep them looking tidy, and the vertical growth of the Leyland cypress is so rapid that it will soon be out of reach of the longest ladder.

Roses look their best against a sober, dense background, and for this yew is incomparable. Relatively slow to develop (but it can be helped along by regular weeding and feeding in its early years), yew needs only one cut a year and can be shaped with great precision to make green architecture in any style from monumental to fantastical. Its matt, light-absorbing texture makes a better background to roses than those plants such as holly, whose leaves glisten and reflect the light, just as indoors matt emulsion paints make a better background to fine pictures than high gloss paint would. Other evergreen shrubs suitable for less formal hedging are escallonia, *Viburnum tinus* and pyracantha which, if not too severely pruned, will provide flowers and, in the case of pyracantha, berries too; Hippophae (sea buckthorn) or *Griselinia littoralis* with its fresh-looking light green leaves both resist salt-laden winds and so are useful by the seaside. Although not evergreen, beech and hornbeam keep their russet leaves throughout the winter, and can be clipped to neat shapes.

Of course, hedges do not have to be green. At Newby Hall there is a delightful little paved and sunken garden of old roses, with philadelphus and carefully chosen and unusual herbaceous plants, enclosed on all four sides by a hedge of purple beech. The same effect could be achieved with *Berberis thunbergii* 'Atro-purpurea' (with the bonus of bright red autumn colour) or *Prunus pissardii* 'Nigra', with pale pink flowers in spring. Good as a hedge, the prunus makes a dull and heavy-looking tree when its very brief flowering season is over, but would be a good host for one of the vigorous, creamy-yellow rambling roses, such as 'Wedding Day', 'Lykkefund' or 'Claire Jacquier'.

Where there is space and a tidy, architectural hedge is not appropriate (perhaps at the boundary between rose garden and orchard or wild garden, or where the garden meets the landscape), a traditional country hedge could be planted, and maintained by laying in the traditional way every five or seven years. With hawthorn as its basis, such a hedge could include some or all of the following: field maple, hazel, holly, elder, blackthorn, willow, oak, ash, beech, gean, guelder rose, wayfarer's tree. Old man's beard (wild clematis), honeysuckle, sweetbriar, wild hop and dog rose could be planted to ramble through it.

If there is some urgency about providing enclosure, for the sake of privacy or to shut out an ugly view, a timber fence can be put up and a hedge planted inside it, with a view to the long term. By the time the hedge has matured, the fence will probably be on its last legs and can be removed. Quick results can also be had from a fence of square-mesh trellis to support quick-growing climbing plants. The mile-a-minute Russian vine (*Polygonum baldschuanicum*) is a desperate last resort as it really grows too fast and its vigour is prodigious. It will knock the trellis over within three years or so. So will *Clematis montana*. Reasonably fast and slightly more moderate in their behaviour are the honey-suckles, *Lonicera japonica* 'Halliana' or *Lonicera periclymenum*; vines such as *Vitis vinifera* 'Brandt' or the claret vine; and *Solanum crispum* 'Glasnevin'. Most rambler roses, too, will cover a fence effectively by their third year. For the first few years, annual climbers could be used to supplement them: runner beans and climbing French beans are decorative as well as edible, and nasturtiums, canary creeper, and *Cobaea scandens* would be equally effective.

The ground plan of any garden or part of a garden usually depends upon one or more unalterable existing feature. The position of the doors of the house will dictate the positions of paths; the shortest route to the kitchen may indicate the best place for a paved area for eating and drinking out of doors. Or such a convenient arrangement may have to be sacrificed in order to catch the last of the evening sun in a corner sheltered from the wind. Perhaps a fine vista from the window of a particular room is the main objective, or perhaps it is important to make a pretty walk from the house to a distant part of the garden. In Britain even the keenest gardeners probably spend more time looking at their garden from a window in the house than walking round it. Moreover, when they are in the garden they are likely to be on their knees weeding, or bent double pruning or hoeing, so that the plants are seen and enjoyed in close-up, leaving the views enjoyed from indoors as the main opportunity to appreciate vistas and the architecture of plants.

Making a plan that accommodates these and other considerations will be like doing a jigsaw puzzle. And there are some additional pieces to add, those simple rules of proportion which can be broken at will, but, nevertheless, are a useful guide. A border should be roughly half as wide as the hedge or wall behind it is tall; anything less looks mean (this rule obviously does not apply if the border is in front of a row of Leyland cypress, when you would end up with one 20ft/7m wide). The proportion of planted areas to paved or turfed areas should be one-third to two-thirds, or a quarter to three-quarters, not half and half. Within a bed or border, unless a two-dimensional pattern on the ground is the objective, the height and bulk of the plants should be varied to avoid monotony; it is particularly important to provide strong planting, in terms of either height or bulk or both, at either end of a long bed.

The ground surface of the rose garden provides a background to the plants that is as important as the hedges, walls or fences that surround it. Grass is perhaps the most satisfying carpet to

'Albertine' provides scent at ground-floor and first-floor windows, Haddon Hall, Derbyshire.

use, the cool, green forming a restful antidote to the dancing colours of the flowers. In a formal garden, lawns and grass walks need to be immaculate: weed-free, mown frequently and close, but not shaved bald, and neatly edged. This entails a good deal of work, but time spent edging lawns can be saved if a 'mowing strip' of paving is laid between beds and turf, set between half and three-quarters of an inch below the level of the turf. In a less formal setting, in a cottage garden, or one where the design is one of informal, exuberant planting within a formal layout, a laxer mowing régime can be adopted; daisies, buttercups and dandelions can be allowed to scatter themselves in the turf providing a pleasant overall texture from a distance, and adding their artless charm in close-up.

Where the planting is completely informal, with shrub and species roses in bold clumps and roses clambering over hedges and into trees, the grass can be allowed to grow long, keeping paths close-mown to provide a dry walk. This will allow a planting of spring bulbs, to give pleasure from late winter when the gallant snowdrops and aconites brave the elements, through till late spring when late tulips and *Gladiolus byzantinus* will overlap with the earliest roses.

In a very small garden, grass may not be a suitable ground cover. Too frequent traffic to and fro can reduce a lawn to a scruffy patch of mud and in a terraced house there is often no convenient place to keep a mower. Too many small town gardens are spoilt by ugly little sheds which are erected to house a machine used to cut a postage-stamp size patch of balding turf. In these circumstances, or when the garden can only be reached by a flight of steps, life is much easier if the ground can be paved.

There are so many materials available for paving that a scheme can be worked out for any scale and any shape of garden. Stone or slate slabs of various sizes, bricks, granite setts, wooden blocks, cobbles, interlocking concrete blocks, tiles, and gravel of different grades can be used alone or in combinations to make patterns which will bring warmth and interest to the garden in the bleak winter months. The choice of paving material will be influenced by traditional local building materials, by the scale and mood of the garden, and by the colour scheme. The problem of growing blue-pink flowers next to brick is less acute with paving than with walls, because the pink of the flowers can be separated from

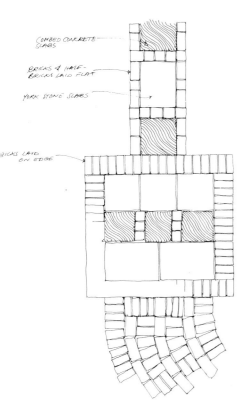

COMBED CONCRETE
SLABS

BRICKS & HALF-
BRICKS LAID FLAT

YORK STONE SLABS

BRICKS LAID
ON EDGE

Varied pattern and texture of a
path at Goodnestone Park,
Kent.

the orange of the brick by other plants. Shrubs with grey or silver
leaves look particularly good against brick. If concrete paving
slabs are used, it is best to avoid those with pink, yellow or green
pigment added to them. They look garishly artificial in any setting,
whereas concrete of a neutral greyish colour can be encouraged
to weather rapidly by the application of sour milk, yoghurt or
diluted manure and will soon attract the lichens and mosses that
give natural stone such a mellow patina.

The cheapest material is gravel; the only snag is that it sticks
to muddy boots. It combines very well with stone and brick, and
can be used to fill the interstices of a brick pattern, as a background
to slabs laid as stepping stones, or to make the transition between
the straight edges of rectangular paving stones and the curved
lines of beds or lawns. Paving can also be used to create optical
illusions. Slabs laid diagonally or brick laid in a herringbone
pattern will make a small space appear larger, and bricks laid in
courses along a path will make it seem longer and narrower,
whereas if the courses run across the path it will seem shorter
and wider.

The harsh formality of newly laid paving can be softened by
planting creeping plants such as chamomile, thymes, campanulas
and pennyroyal in the cracks between the stones. Thyme and
chamomile, in particular, do not mind being stepped on occasionally and when crushed will release their scent, giving added pleasure. By planting chamomile roots six to nine inches apart in
gravel, a sward dense enough to be called a lawn can be achieved
in a few years. It needs thorough and frequent weeding in the
early stages, but the scent is so delightful that weeding becomes
a pleasure. It is a mistake to seal the joints between paving stones
with mortar, as the mortar starts to crack and crumble with the
first hard frost. If hand-weeding is too time-consuming, it is
better to leave the joints unplanted and apply an annual dose of
weedkiller.

The width of a paved terrace immediately in front of the house
should be half the height of the house to make a well-
proportioned, visually stable base and, in general, the proportions
of a rectangular area are most pleasing if the width can be half,
quarter, two-thirds or one-third of the length. A terrace for eating
and drinking out of doors should be paved with brick, stone or
concrete, as table and chair legs will sink in grass or gravel, and

enough space should be allowed for chairs to be pushed back from the table.

There are practical rules, too, for planning paths. A hard surface is essential for paths which receive a lot of traffic; the erosion of grass paths by the feet of thousands of visitors is a serious problem to the National Trust in gardens like Sissinghurst and Hidcote, and the same problem can arise in a private garden even if there are only two or three pairs of feet using the path once or twice a day. A paved path provides another opportunity to make patterns, the materials used and the patterns formed depending upon the relationship of the path to the house and to other parts of the garden. A change in the texture and pattern of a path can also mark a change in character between one part of the garden and another.

Paths are, of course, functional first and decorative only second. Their function is to take you, and possibly your garden machinery, from one place to another safely and by the most direct route. A path should always lead somewhere, whether it is to the potting shed, the swimming pool, the orchard or a seat under a shady tree. Purposeless paths which peter out into nothing are irritating. If the design of the garden requires a vista along a path which leads to a dead end, finishing, perhaps, against a boundary wall, the path can be given a purpose by placing a seat at its end. Similarly, however romantic the notion of a serpentine path may seem, its meandering will lead to nothing but frustration when you are pushing a wheelbarrow full of bindweed to the bonfire. If the serpentine route has an aesthetic purpose, concealing and revealing pictures within the garden, sense can be made of its twists and turns by placing obstacles along the way: a tree here, a dense clump of shrubs there.

The minimum width of a path along which two people can walk comfortably side by side is 4ft/1.2m if the path is open on both sides, and 6½ft/2m if the path is enclosed by hedges or walls. It is frustrating to have to walk round a garden in single file. These widths will also accommodate most garden machinery. This is a rule to break if an atmosphere of intimacy is required, and if plants like lavender, santolina and rosemary are to release the fragrance of their aromatic leaves as the passer-by brushes against them it may be worth the discomfort of wet legs after rain.

Above A simple but elegant timber fence and weathered brick paving enhance a planting of yellow roses and *Stachys olympica* at Bodnant, North Wales.

Below Between hedges of 'Rosa Mundi', a grass path at Kiftsgate leads invitingly towards a statue framed by a whitebeam arch.

On a slope, paved paths can become dangerously slippery and gravel will be washed down the slope in heavy rain, so there should be steps rather than a bank if the gradient is steeper than one in twelve. Broad, shallow steps, measured in strides rather than feet, can be surfaced with the same material as the path, and edged with brick, stone or timber. In the wilder parts of the garden simple steps can be made in a path of grass, gravel or crushed bark by laying down railway sleepers or half larch poles and driving in pegs to hold them in position.

A gradient steeper than one in three always requires a flight of steps. Gertrude Jekyll hated the sight of a grass bank; she thought it ugly, and considered it a missed opportunity to build a retaining wall over which Scottish roses could tumble. Alternatively, the roses could be planted directly into the bank. Some of the new 'ground cover' roses would be ideal in such a situation. Steps, whether they are flanked by a bank or by retaining walls, are all too often built to uncomfortable dimensions. The risers are too steep and the treads too narrow, so that they are not only hazardous to negotiate but also cramped in appearance. If space permits, risers should be no higher than 6in/150mm, treads should be a generous 14in/360mm wide, and if more than seven steps are needed to complete the climb, they should be divided, with a resting platform between. Changes of level in a garden offer all sorts of exciting opportunities to the designer, not least in the design of flights of steps, for of course steps do not have to charge straight up a slope. They can rise parallel to the slope, or be angled or curved into the slope or out from the slope, or partly out, partly in, like Lutyens' elegant steps at Marsh Court, The Hoo and Ashby St Ledgers. Lutyens' skill in devising graceful ways of changing levels, his paving patterns, and his smooth progressions from one axial direction to another are illustrated in Jane Brown's book on the partnership of Lutyens and Miss Jekyll, *Gardens of a Golden Afternoon*.

So far I have considered only two of the elements of which the landscape is composed: plants and stone. The third is water. If the aim in making a garden is to take the elements of landscape and adapt and rearrange them so as to make a beautiful place, a garden is surely incomplete if one of the elements is left out. If you take away stone, what is Stourhead without its temples and bridges? Take away plants, and try to imagine the Villa d'Este without trees to shade its walks, mosses to drape its stone basins, and ferns to soften its massive walls. Try filling the canals and fountains at Versailles with bedding plants instead of water. These are examples on a grand scale, but the principle also applies to quite modest gardens, and still applies whether the garden in question aims at distilling the essence of nature or at manipulating nature to produce a theatrical fantasy.

Each element has its unique properties and one of the delights of gardening is to try and use those properties to the full. One of the entrancing properties of water is its ability to reflect: to lay the sky at our feet, to turn the arc of a bridge into a circle, to present to the overhanging flower or branch its own image.

Then there is the power of movement that water possesses, shown in the surface of a pond slightly ruffled by a breeze, the sparkling droplets or gushing jet of a fountain, and the torrential rush of a weir. Water can touch the emotions not only through the eye but also through the ear, soothing the spirits with the gurgling of a stream, or uplifting them with the crashing of a cascade.

In the rose garden, water can be used both for its own sake and to enhance the mood of the planting: a somnolent, still pool to match the sleepy opulence of full-petalled, richly coloured Bourbon and Hybrid Perpetual roses; gaily sparkling fountains imitating the arching of weeping standards in a garden of multi-coloured roses arranged in the French style, or a cascade echoing in its fall the fall of 'The Garland' or 'Wedding Day' from an old pear tree above the pond.

Natural water in a garden is a great blessing. Where there is a stream or a spring to feed it, a pond or lake will follow the contours and appear convincingly natural. At Cholmondley Castle there is just such a lake, with 'Wedding Day' arching over the water at one side; on the opposite bank *R. paulii* falls towards the water among drifts of blue and white irises backed by a clump of five *R.* 'Cantabrigiensis'. The view across the lake to the park is framed by a bold group of some fifteen 'Nevada' on one side and as many 'Frühlingsgold' on the other, with a dark background of *Prunus laurocerasus* with forest trees beyond, and a foreground of hostas and *Alchemilla mollis*.

CHAPTER TEN

The Framework

... The garden of Pleasure is to be set about with arbours, covered with jessamine, musk roses, myrtle trees, bay trees, woodbine, vines, sweet bryer and other rare things....

Gervase Markham, *The Countrie Farm*

The vertical dimension is not always given enough consideration in garden planning. Very often, it is the one thing that is lacking in an otherwise satisfactory garden. A garden should surround the viewer. It should be not only at our feet but beside and above us as well. In the most beautiful rose gardens, one can always look up to roses as well as down upon them: they arch and cascade out of trees, they lure the visitor through tunnels of colour and scent, and roses trained upwards present their flowers at eye and nose level to be enjoyed for their perfection of form and their sweet fragrance.

The structures for displaying climbing and rambling roses are legion. A rose arch spanning a path or framing a door can be charming, but it can also be unpleasingly quaint. To avoid this the site, the material used and the shape of the arch must be chosen with care. The arch must have a purpose. If it is placed inconsequentially it will look silly and become an irritation. Rather, it should span a gap in a hedge or wall, giving importance to the passage from one part of the garden to another; or it may be set against a wall to frame a sculpture or urn; two arches crossing each other can mark the crossing of two paths, and other, more complex arrangements of arches can be made where paths meet.

The material from which an arch is constructed will depend upon the architecture of house and garden, and also the style of the garden. Ready-made arches are available of metal, sawn timber, rustic poles and timber or wire trellis-work. With a few exceptions, ready-made arches are always built too small, so that roses trained on them are likely to scratch your eyes out and rip your clothes. The minimum acceptable width is $4\frac{1}{2}$ft/1.3m for one person to pass through unscathed, and 7ft/2m for two, and the height of the arch should be at least $7\frac{1}{2}$ft/2.2m. Metal, although

The rustic pergola at Polesden Lacey, Surrey, forms a tunnel of roses.

susceptible to rust, is more enduring than timber which is subject to rot.

The material used will also dictate the shape of the arch to some extent. Rustic poles cannot be bent into curves, so a rustic arch of peeled or unpeeled poles will either have a flat top at right angles to the sides or a triangular, gabled top. The latter never looks quite right, whereas a straight top, strengthened by a diagonal timber in the angle of its joint with the upright posts, makes a satisfying shape, either as a double arch or in a series to form a tunnel, as at Polesden Lacey. The structure must be sturdy enough to support the weight of the roses and so, for the sake of strength (both structural and visual), a double arch, with the two pieces joined with horizontal bars, is usually preferable to a single. However, a series of single arches joined side by side can make an elegant division between two parts of the garden.

A metal arch, if it is to span a width of 7ft/2m or more, is often better topped with a flattened arch than with a complete semi-circle. If the arch is sprung from uprights that are, say 6ft/1.8m high, a semi-circular arc would be 9½ft/2.8m from the ground at its apex, giving rather too much height for any but the grandest garden. The most graceful arches are made from flat metal bent on edge, rather than from metal tubing or flat metal bent on its narrow plane. Roses du Temps Passé in Staffordshire supply arches constructed by this method which are in suitably generous dimensions.

The weight of a robust climbing rose in full bloom is considerable, and the elegant, airy effect of wire mesh arches is lost when they become buckled by the weight of the plants they were intended to support. They are as fragile in structure as they are in appearance. Wooden trellis, too, unless it is made to sturdier dimensions than are usually seen is not sufficiently durable.

A row of arches at regular intervals forms a tunnel, and a double row of pillars joined by wooden beams and cross-bars makes a pergola. In both cases the purpose is the same: to provide a shaded walk from one point to another. Like all paths in the garden, the path under a pergola should lead somewhere. There should also be a barrier on each side, either of plants or in the form of a low wall, so that one is forced to take the path beneath it: a pergola marching across the middle of a lawn is pointless because there is nothing to prevent one walking round it instead

Above Pruning and tying in climbing roses on an arched arbour. *The Gardener's Labyrinth* by Thomas Hill (1586).

Below A Victorian rose arch.

of through it. The arches of the tunnel or the cross-bars of the pergola should be far enough apart to allow light in, otherwise the roses will grow exclusively upwards towards the light and the aim, a tunnel of flowers, will be defeated. It is also important that light should filter down on to the path, or a grass path will soon turn to sludge and a paved path to mossy slime. It is, in any case, best to avoid using flagstones as they can become dangerously slippery in a shaded walk. Gravel or brick paving is safer.

Gertrude Jekyll wrote that a pergola should never turn and twist, but the approach to the rose garden at Warwick Castle through the gently curving tunnel of roses, which conceals the garden until you are almost in it, is most effective. There is another splendid curved pergola at Bodnant in north Wales, constructed of airy but robust timber trellis-work and planted with climbing roses and *Solanum crispum* 'Glasnevin'. The path beneath is bordered with *Libertia formosa* followed by pink Japanese anemones.

A rose garden with any pretensions to romance must have an arbour or bower. 'The simple old Rose arbour,' writes Miss Jekyll, 'by no means so often seen as it might well be, should be in every modest garden.' Queen Elizabeth I used the arbours in the gardens of Hampton Court to consult her advisers and they were also, perhaps, the scene of more romantic assignations: 'Love-thoughts lie rich when canopied with bowers.' A little earlier Bishop Bonner used the privacy of an arbour at Fulham Palace for a more dubious purpose when, supposedly in order to persuade a young heretic to recant, the zealous Bishop 'having him to his orchard, there, within a little arbour, with his own hands beat him with a willow wand.'

Nowadays, when there is always so much to be done in the garden, an arbour needs to be very inviting indeed for the gardener to be able to enjoy its tranquillity without being assailed by feelings of guilt about tasks neglected. A simple arbour is easily constructed in the angle of a wall, like the one in the little walled garden at Westbury Court in Gloucestershire planted with vines. Gertrude Jekyll's suggestion for a simple arbour was to construct a wide, deep arch, backed with a hedge or yew or box, and train a 'Dundee Rambler' over the top with 'Aimée Vibert' or an Alba rose to the other side.

An arbour can be as simple or as elaborate as you care to make

OVERLEAF

Left The luxuriant rambler 'Ethel' forms the background to the tranquil pool at the RNRS's gardens near St. Albans. A massed planting of 'The Fairy' repeats the theme in the foreground.

Right:

Above An intricate bamboo pergola supports *Rosa banksiae* at Canglangting Garden, Suzhou, China.

Below Weeping standards give height in a border at Monet's Giverny garden.

it. The important requirements are that it should be in a secluded, sheltered place, out of earshot of the telephone or doorbell, and that it should be constructed from plants. It is intended as a green enclosure, and if the built framework is more in evidence than the plants, it ceases to be an arbour and becomes a summer house, gazebo or pavilion. At Moseley Old Hall in Staffordshire, the wooden arbour illustrated in Thomas Hill's *A Gardener's Labyrinth* (1577) has been copied, planted not with roses but with clematis and vines. Among the prettiest of rose arbours are those in the Potager at Villandry, where arched, wooden latticed alcoves covered in roses punctuate the vegetable parterre.

With patience, an arbour can be made from a single plant. A tall, weeping standard, trained to form a wide-arching umbrella, or a climber trained to a strong central post and treated in the same way will, in time, form a secret bower with the arching shoots reaching to the ground and room inside for a seat. Suitable roses include 'Adélaide d'Orléans' and 'Félicité et Perpétue', both' with pink buds opening to white, both scented and both nearly evergreen; 'Amadis' (the Crimson Boursault) and 'Violette' which have the advantage of being thornless; 'Bleu Magenta' for its opulent colouring; 'Débutante', the best pink rambler; 'Francis E. Lester', pink fading to white; 'Kew Rambler', with trusses of single light pink flowers, followed by small orange hips; or 'Phyllis Bide' with her rare colouring of soft, pale orangey-yellow.

There are many ways of using roses to provide vertical interest in the garden for both formal and informal effects. Modern climbing roses of the Hybrid Tea and Floribunda types tend to be stiff in their habit of growth and are best trained against a wall or trellis with shrubs or less vigorous twiners planted in front to conceal their gaunt, ungainly legs. Rambler roses, on the other hand, put out long, flexible stems each season which arch freely and are at their best trained upwards to the required height, then allowed to cascade freely downwards, hiding the supporting structure.

The structure used depends on the height, width and degree of formality required. In the wild garden, a stout larch post or, better still but seldom available, a dead tree with its top taken off at a height of anything between 8–10ft/2.4–3m will do the job well. To be completely stable in the ground, posts should be planted with at least a quarter of their length buried, the under-

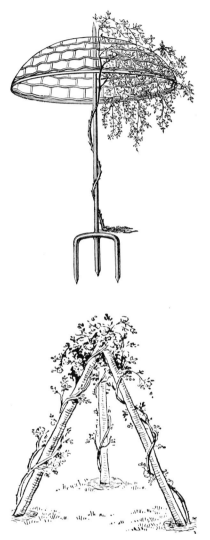

Victorian supports for climbing roses.

ground part thoroughly soaked in a wood preserver and preferably bedded in concrete. To give the effect of a wide, gracefully arching shrub, three ramblers of the same variety can be planted within a structure of four posts splaying outwards and joined at their tops with horizontal bars. In an informal setting, this vase-shaped outline has a more natural appearance than the alternative, which is a tripod or square-based pyramidal structure narrowing towards the top.

Today we are rather pusillanimous about using plants in artificial ways, fearing lest our efforts should be considered to be in bad taste. When I was studying landscape architecture, symmetrical garden plans were despised, and squares and circles banished in favour of random, free-flowing shapes (although hexagons and octagons, were considered rather chic); and flowers, particularly roses, were frowned upon. It was not thought right to torture any plant, even the despised rose, into unnatural shapes. But it seems a pity not to take advantage of the rose's amiable responsiveness to training. There is room in the garden to show elegant artificiality alongside natural exuberance, in such a way that the contrast is exciting and appropriate to the setting.

One of the most delightfully graceful and flamboyant ways to display climbing roses which have long and flexible stems is to make swags and festoons by training them along ropes or chains slung between posts. Chain, heavier than rope, hangs better, and the symmetry of its arc is less likely to be distorted by the weight of the roses. In the rose garden at Bagatelle, the chains are bound closely with stout cord, so that the rose stems are not damaged by rubbing against the metal. In an elaborately formal garden, an avenue or division between two areas could be made by alternating swags with arches, giving a vertically serpentine effect. A weeping standard could be grown under each arch, or roses trained to a spherical metal structure to form a 'balloon', a method described by Gertrude Jekyll in *Roses for English Gardens*.

A point to remember when training climbing roses or shrub roses with flexible shoots is that, if the stems can be bent or arched to a horizontal or downward-pointing position, buds will break all the way along the stems, giving greater freedom of flowering. This is easy enough to achieve when training roses to horizonal wires on a large, blank wall, but not so simple on a house wall where windows intervene. On a house, the rose can either be planted directly under a window and trained out and then up to frame the window, or planted between windows and trained upwards until clear of the ground-floor windows, then bent out horizontally between ground and first floor. Roses grown beneath or beside windows should be chosen for their scent.

The bending over of shoots of shrub roses is known as 'pegging down', the flexible shoots being secured to short pegs pushed into the ground. The same effect can be obtained by fixing a panel of square trellis of the required size horizontally about 9in/22cm above the ground, and tying the shoots to it.

There is almost limitless scope for achieving different effects by training roses in the various ways outlined above; roses, more than any other shrub or climbing plant, provide opportunities for vertical gardening where growing space is restricted and I hope that owners of small gardens, besides those with plenty of space to fill, may be inspired to try some of these methods.

The furnishings in a garden can make or mar it. 'By 'furnishings' I mean not only seats and tables, but also pots, urns and statuary: ornaments introduced into the rose garden either for their own decorative qualities, in order to complement the roses, or as containers for the plants.

For the lazy gardener there are two criteria for garden seats: first that they should be comfortable (to sit on) because the lazy gardener prefers to sit and look at the garden than to get up and weed it; secondly, that they should be weatherproof, so that they can stay out all the year round. Fortunately the latter rules out anything with garishly upholstered seats on a plastic frame: that kind of furniture can stay by the swimming pool, out of sight of the rose garden.

Unless you are attempting a strict reconstruction of a period garden, it seems a pity to buy reproductions of old designs when there is an opportunity to encourage today's craftsmen but, sadly, it is not easy to find well-designed, well-made modern garden furniture. Nevertheless, it is worth seeking out the local Craft Guild if there is one, or even searching the telephone directory for garden furniture makers, blacksmiths or wrought iron workers. Unless you are lucky enough to discover an inspired designer, it is best to choose a simple, sturdy design on conventional lines. For those who lack the confidence or the cash to

Above An arbour of robust timber construction.

Below Climbing roses supported on arched metal frames at the Albert Kahn Garden, Paris. Simple, elegant bench seats are painted blue-black.

commission work, there are several reliable makers of pieces which have become classics, such as the Lutyens seat with its gracefully curving back and Charles Verey's Country Garden seat which makes reference to Chinese Chippendale.

In a small, paved garden, or a roof garden, or on a balcony, roses can be grown in containers. On roofs and balconies it is as well to be sure that the structure is strong enough to bear the weight of containers full of wet soil or compost. Plastic containers are to be avoided: their very lightness, which might seem an advantage, is a liability, as a plant of any size in a plastic pot will be top-heavy and blow over in the lightest wind. The bigger the pot, the better the rose planted in it will thrive, but some roses are remarkably brave, and even climbing roses can be grown in pots and will embellish railings or trellis (for suitable varities, see Appendix B). Large pots usually look better than small ones, even in quite small spaces. Those which look substantial in the pottery or garden centre seem to have shrunk by the time one gets them home. Large, traditional flower pots, or well-rounded bowls made of terracotta look good; they are better without elaborate ornamentation and excrescences if they are to contain plants. Some garden centres sell the glazed Chinese pots in which pickled eggs are imported; they are coloured a neutral, sludgy beige-green, and usually decorated with a sinuous dragon chasing its tail around the pot. There is also a wide choice of pots made of re-constituted stone, which are acceptable if chosen carefully: those with a smooth surface or with obvious signs of artificial pigment are to be avoided. It is best to choose ones which already have a colour and texture close to that of natural stone. They soon weather if left for a season in a damp, shady place, and weathering can be helped along with applications of sour milk or diluted manure.

Traditional wooden Versailles tubs are excellent containers for broad-headed or weeping standard roses in a rather grand setting. For a small roof or balcony, wooden containers specially made in dimensions to suit the site are also useful. Custom-built wooden troughs can incorporate trellis panels or pyramids to support climbing roses and other climbing plants; if set on casters, they can easily be moved around. Movable pots and tubs provide scope for altering the appearance of the garden from week to week (or even day to day). If limited space dictates that plants can be grown only in containers, some pots of box clipped into globes, pyramids and cones will provide solid shapes to contrast with the loose, shrubby form of the roses.

Painted wooden or metal furniture, tubs, fencing, gates, doors and trellis work raises the question of colour. White seems to be the most popular colour in gardens, but I am not at all sure that it is the best. In some gardens it is too glaring and obtrusive; it distracts from the subtleties of plant colour combinations and prevents the eye being drawn to a distant view. Very pale bluish grey will seem almost as crisp as white without being as dazzling.

If a camouflage effect is required where, for example, supports for plants are necessary but should be invisible or a fence is necessary but must not interrupt the view, black is, surprisingly, the most unobtrusive colour. It is nearly always a mistake to use green paint in the garden. 'Park Bench' green, especially, appears dead and harsh against the living greens of grass and leaves. Khaki is reasonably effective camouflage for garden gates and seats as for soldiers, and very dark green or navy blue look elegant in a formal context.

Colour need not always be so discreet. There is a shade of blue-green, almost peacock blue, introduced by Charles Wade to his garden at Snowshill (now owned by the National Trust) and imitated in several other gardens. It is a strong, pleasing colour, but perhaps not flattering to roses with blue or purple in their colouring. Out of respect for the roses one should also avoid using dramatically strong colours, though in general I feel there is too little spirit of adventure about the use of colour in the garden. In San Francisco the woodwork on a Japanese teahouse is painted a scarlet that would lift the spirits if seen through a grey English drizzle, but I have not come across anything as bold in Britain. Scarlet would not do for the rose garden; there one might well settle for navy blue or for a particular shade of blue-grey with a purplish warmth to it. I first saw this colour used in the Tate Gallery some time ago. It impressed me then as a warm neutral colour which had the effect of enhancing the colours in the paintings displayed against it, and it seems to have the same beneficial relationship with flower and foliage colours in the garden.

CHAPTER ELEVEN

The Roses

She's a voluptuary, think of her
Wine-dark and heavy-scented of the South . . .
. . . deep and old and cunning in deceit,
Offering promises too near the thorn . . .
She plays the madrigal when moist with dew
To charm the English in their artless few.
But at her wiser older broad remove
Remains an Asiatic and a Roman,
Accomplice of the centuries and love.

Vita Sackville-West, *The Garden*

When it comes to choosing the roses for the rose garden, we are faced with an *embarras de richesse*. What we need is a system of elimination. Gertrude Jekyll would have started by banishing all roses of deep crimson and purple colouring: she did not care for their opulence and wrote, 'A Rose garden can never be called gorgeous; the term is quite unfitting.' But it would be a pity, in doing away with 'gorgeous' roses, to forgo Vita Sackville-West's wine-dark voluptuaries.

Since we must start somewhere, let us rule out roses without scent, unless their other qualities are so outstanding that one cannot bear to be without them. Because we don't have time to administer the weekly dose of fungicide – and because even when we do, it does not always work – we can eliminate all roses which are martyrs to blackspot and mildew. Goodbye, 'Dorothy Perkins'; 'Zéphirine Drouhin', get back to your north wall. I would also banish any roses of weak constitution, those with heads too heavy for their stems, and those which disappoint in wet weather, their buds turning to soggy brown lumps before they can open. In the modern rose garden there is no place either for roses that do not form a reasonably shapely shrub. On these grounds, out would go many Hybrid Tea roses, and many of the Hybrid Perpetuals bred by Victorian and Edwardian rosarians for bigger, more shapely show blooms at the expense of their performance as flowering shrubs.

I place emphasis on healthy growth and well-formed shrubs

Rosa complicata at Mottisfont Abbey.

because it is obviously important that the plants should thrive and that they should make their contribution as good garden plants as well as producing beautiful flowers. Others may have different criteria. A long flowering season may be their priority, in which case they will look first for roses which flower 'continuously' or at all events are 'repeat flowering'. Usually those plants which put their effort into keeping up their display over a long period bear fewer flowers at a time than those which have one glorious flowering for a comparatively short time. I am happy to sacrifice the longer season for the stunning spectacle of a shrub smothered and weighted down with its burden of blooms. I enjoy observing seasonal changes in the garden and I do not want to look at the same rose month after month, any more than I want to eat asparagus and raspberries all the year round.

So, whilst perpetual flowering roses have great value in the garden, others should not be abandoned simply because they flower in one glorious burst. Greater care spent planning for a succession of roses and judicious interplanting of other shrubs and herbaceous plants can have rewarding results. The early flowering yellow species roses and their hybrids such as *Rosa* 'Cantabrigiensis', *R. pimpinellifolia* and its hybrids 'Frühlingsgold' and 'Frühlingsmorgen', with their simple flowers and fresh colouring, make an appropriate transition from spring to summer, when the more luscious Albas, Gallicas, Damasks and Bourbons come into their own, some of the latter flowering intermittently right through till the first frosts. In mid-summer, just when most of the old roses begin to fade, the Hybrid Musks come into their own and prolong the rose season into the autumn when large trusses of flowers bloom on vigorous new growth.

The different shapes and sizes of flowers provide scope for creating harmonies and contrasts. The little pompom flowers of a group of 'Little White Pet' or 'Swany' planted at the feet of 'Madame Hardy' or 'Boule de Neige' will contrast prettily with the full, sophisticated flowers of the larger shrub. The same effect could be achieved in pink with 'Nozomi' underlying 'Souvenir de la Malmaison', or 'Fantin-Latour'. Roses with single flowers make a pleasing contrast to doubles of the same colour; 'Golden Wings', for example, with 'Graham Thomas'.

Another combination along the same lines would be to plant the climber 'Meg' with her large, soft apricot, almost single flowers alongside 'Dream Girl', 'Schoolgirl' or 'Compassion'. At the foot of their wall I would use apricot and buff Hybrid Musks with a background of purple-leaved cotinus, and perhaps add a group of 'White Wings', breaking my scent rule for its lovely single flowers with their unusual red stamens, and a foreground group of neat little 'Gruss an Aachen' which has pretty flowers of old-rose shape, flesh coloured, fading to cream. Then I would look for more coppery-purple foliage, to rescue the soft colour scheme from insipidity: *Berberis thunbergii* 'Atropurpurea Nana', perhaps, or *Heuchera americana* or *Saxifraga fortunei* 'Wada'. A spikey phormium or the flowers of *Salvia superba* 'May Night' would add vertical emphasis.

It is easier to succeed with limited, soft colour combinations, but to experiment with more adventurous schemes gives greater satisfaction when they succeed. What a triumph to get orange and purple into the same bed and make it look as if their marriage was made in heaven. I have not seen this done with roses, but Monet achieved it in his garden at Giverny using (as far as I can tell from a postcard of his painting of the scene, which burns and sings with colour) orange nasturtiums and purple asters, with touches here and there of something white. Most of us seem to be pusillanimous about colour, perhaps because we are afraid of revealing Bad Taste if we are too bold. Take courage from Penelope Hobhouse's book *Colour in Your Garden*: she gives a lucid analysis of colour principles and goes on to give her own creative ideas about using plant colours to enhance each other and to make well-planned combinations. Gertrude Jekyll's *Colour Schemes for the Flower Garden* is also full of inspiration.

Colour in roses encompasses every hue in the spectrum with the exception of blue, and even blue is present by stealth in some shades of pink and purple. To plan the planting of a rose garden so that the many shades of white, yellow, orange, pink and purple are seen in such a way that each shade enhances and intensifies, and none detracts from its neighbour, is no mean challenge. The dangers are that delicate tints will appear bleached out by their harsher neighbours, subtle tones be muddied by juxtaposition with clear tints. The lilac, grey and violet that are all present in 'Jeanne Duval' (called after the mistress of Baudelaire) would be lost beside a clear red rose.

Incompatible colours can be kept apart by interposing white

roses or other plants, or linked by using plants of a colour sympathetic to both. Plants with coppery-purple or grey foliage are particularly useful for this purpose. Where there is space, *Rosa glauca* (formerly called *Rosa rubrifolia*) is perfect, the fleeting appearance of its single pink flowers being compensated for by its pinkish-bluish-grey leaves. Most shades of green, too, are effective in separating the subtle colours from the bright, and the salmons from the blue-pinks. Long borders can be divided into bays by yew buttresses, each bay containing roses from a different colour grouping or, in a formally laid out garden, the colour groups can be planted each in its own bed with box, lavender or santolina edgings limiting the sphere of influence of each colour.

The magical atmosphere that used to pervade Vita Sackville-West's White Garden at Sissinghurst has spawned numerous imitations, and not only white gardens but pink gardens, yellow gardens, red gardens and blue borders have sprung up in its wake. Few even begin to approach the success of the original and, with roses, to use one colour only is to deny yourself the pleasure of an almost infinite variety of combinations. The problem is to arrive at colour combinations that will make the rose garden into something that is more than a pleasant scene of well-chosen harmonies and contrasts. Perhaps the best way to set about achieving it is to take a limited group of roses, either by colour (pink, yellow and white, for example, or crimson, purple and striped) or by class (Alba roses, perhaps, or Gallicas and Bourbons) and to add to and build upon that group to intensify the mood that the group suggests. From the many possibilities I will take just three examples: a garden based on roses of pale, fresh colours, Albas, China roses and Noisettes, to develop a mood of romantic tranquillity; a garden of bright, clear colours, with an atmosphere of gaiety; and a third garden of the voluptuous and seductive roses described in the poem at the beginning of this chapter.

The first imaginary example, the romantic rose garden, would be, perhaps, quite small, enclosed by hedges or walls, and paved with brick or stone. It would certainly have an arbour in a corner or against a wall, sheltering a seat from the midday sun but catching the sun's late afternoon warmth. A still, stone-edged pool, or one of Gertrude Jekyll's rills, through which the water gurgles invisibly, like Tennyson's 'brooks of Eden mazily mur-

The White Border in the Fountain Garden at Tintinhull, Somerset: *Malva moschata* 'Alba', *Santolina virens* and *Lychnis coronaria* 'Alba' are among the plants which provide varied shapes and textures.

muring', would be soothing. The roses themselves would be chosen for their air of fragility and, for contrast, they would be surrounded with solid, low walls of box, lavender or santolina. Shrub and herbaceous planting to enhance the roses would include soft blues (not the clear blue of forget-me-nots or anchusas) and mauves, leaving out bright pink and yellow, and avoiding the acid greenish-yellow of those shrubs that are mis-described as having 'golden' foliage.

And what of the roses? Albas, Chinas and Noisettes all have flowers of delicate appearance with modestly pretty colouring, which would suit the gentle mood that is intended. The Alba roses also have very satisfactory foliage, healthy and prolific, and, in Alba 'Maxima', 'Celestial', 'Great Maiden's Blush' and 'Madame Plantier', the leaves have a milky bloom. The colour range of the flowers goes from white through palest blush to the stronger, but never hard pinks of 'Celestial' and 'Queen of Denmark'. One cannot be immune to the romantic associations of the Alba roses: Alba 'Maxima' has been grown since the early Middle Ages, and is also known as the White Rose of York, the Jacobite Rose and Bonnie Prince Charlie's Rose; 'Celestial' is said to have been one of Henry VIII's favourite roses at Hampton Court; and 'Great Maiden's Blush', which was grown in monastery gardens in the fifteenth century and earlier, has also been called 'Cuisse de Nymphe', 'Incarnata', 'La Virginale' and 'La Séduisante'. It would be interesting to know by which names the monks were permitted to call it.

The same delicate flesh pink that is found in some of the Albas also colours 'Cécile Brunner'. There is nothing like its perfect miniature scrolled buds and, in its climbing form, it is vigorous enough to cover an arbour. Its scent, however, is faint and elusive. More vigorous than the bush 'Cécile Brunner', but otherwise similar, is the shrub 'Bloomfield Abundance'. 'Perle d'Or' is identical in all respects except for its colour, which is well described as golden pearl. Many of the China roses are too strongly coloured to include in this particular garden, but 'Parson's Pink China' is silvery pink, strongly scented and nearly thornless, and can make a shrub or reach up to 8 ft/2·4 m on a wall or pillar. 'Sophie's Perpetual' will do the same. I don't care for its rather parti-coloured look, pale pink overlaid with cerise, but I grow it for the same reason that I grow 'Robert le Diable',

'Master Hugh' and 'Janet's Pride' in other parts of the garden: the names of these roses include the Christian names of members of my family, and 'when this you see, remember me' adds to the pleasure of gardening, in the same way that plants that were given by friends do, even if they clash inconveniently with the colour scheme.

The Noisette roses, all climbers with easily trained, flexible stems and abundant foliage, tend to have flowers which are richly coloured in the bud and fade to palest creamy pink ('Blush Noisette'), creamy pale yellow ('Céline Forestier', 'Alister Stella Gray', 'Claire Jacquier', 'Rêve d'Or') or apricot-peach ('Desprez à Fleur Jaune'). 'Aimée Vibert' opens white from pink-tipped buds, and the much-loved 'Gloire de Dijon', Dean Hole's favourite rose, and related to the Noisettes, is a tantalising mixture of buff and apricot. Another relation, 'Madame Alfred Carrière', with larger, full, blush-white flowers, is one of the trustiest of climbers, floriferous and perpetual. Any of these could grace the walls of the romantic rose garden or, with the support of tripod or tall vase, form an arching shrub as the centrepiece in a bed.

If space permitted, I would add the pink ramblers, 'May Queen', 'Kew Rambler' (single flowers), and 'Adélaide d'Orléans' to hang their clusters of small flowers from arbour or arch; the creamy, sweet-scented rambler 'Albéric Barbier'; and 'Sombreuil' for its lovely, quartered white flowers. Shrub roses would include 'Madame Hardy' and 'Boule de Neige' and the compact little pink Centifolias, 'Petite de Hollande' and 'de Meaux'. I would allow a few modern roses that make good shrubs, particularly David Austin's English Roses such as 'Wife of Bath' and 'Heritage', and the Floribundas 'Escapade' with its clusters of nearly single flowers), 'Chanelle', 'Gruss an Aachen' and 'Pink Parfait'. The colours in this garden are all gentle, the bright hard reds and yellows, and the rich crimsons and purples being excluded.

The bright colours come into their own in the second example, where they are chosen to express *joie de vivre*. This garden is intended to lift jaded spirits, and to sparkle with light and colour on the dullest day. This is the place for the controlled exuberance of weeping standards, pillar roses, garlands and swags. The roses will provide a kaleidoscopic confusion of colour, so the cool, refreshing background of green lawns is essential to provide a restful contrast for the eye. The background and means of enclos-

OVERLEAF
Roses for a romantic garden:

Above 'Mme Grégoire Staechelin' framing a doorway at Jenkyn Place, Hampshire.

Below left The subtly coloured, quartered flowers of 'Gloire de Dijon' at Mottisfont Abbey.

Below right The creamy single flowers of 'Nevada' frame a glimpse of a stone figure.

ure too, should, if possible, be green and sober: a yew hedge is ideal. Water would vie with the roses, in the form of fountains of sparkling droplets, or a stream babbling merrily over a bed of shining pebbles.

The colours of the roses are bright and clear reds and yellows, set off by plenty of white. The soft shades of blush, peach and apricot used in the romantic garden would be lost in such a scheme, and the heavy dark crimsons and purplish reds would appear dull and murky.

For weeping standards I would use 'Excelsa', also known as 'Red Dorothy Perkins', a clear, bright crimson rambler which continues flowering all summer; 'Crimson Showers', which is similar but a deeper crimson, or 'Hiawatha', crimson with a white centre. There are plenty of white ramblers to choose from as weeping standards: 'Félicité et Perpétue', 'Albéric Barbier', 'Sanders White' and 'Snow Carpet' are all spectacular, and 'Félicité et Perpétue' will flower in light shade; 'Albéric Barbier', after its main flowering, produces scattered flowers until autumn. It is worth remembering that almost any rose can be grafted to form a standard and many nurseries will undertake this to order. For a weeping standard the rose chosen should be one that has naturally graceful, flexible, arching stems. Many shrub roses will form standards which, while they do not weep, are elegant in habit. The early, single yellow 'Canary Bird', the Hybrid Musk 'Ballerina' with large trusses of single, pink and white flowers, and its red-and-white sister 'Marjorie Fair' would all be ideal for the colourful garden we are planning here. Half-standards, too, with a stem about 3 ft/1 m tall, can be used to vary the height in formal plantings. 'Little White Pet', 'The Fairy', 'De Meaux' and David Austin's 'Yellow Button' all make pretty little mop-heads.

To train on pillars, or against walls and fences up to about 8 ft/2·4 m, a choice could be made between the Hybrid Musks 'Moonlight' and 'Pax', climbing 'Iceberg', pink-edged 'Handel' and 'Swan Lake' among white roses; 'Lawrence Johnston', climbing 'Allgold', the very floriferous and perpetual 'Golden Showers' and 'Leverkusen' for yellow; and among reds, 'Altissimo' with brilliant single flowers, the true red, nearly single 'Parkdirektor Riggers', and crimson-scarlet 'Paul's Scarlet Climber' which has held its great popularity since it first appeared in 1916. For the

PREVIOUS PAGE
Roses for exuberant colour:

Above 'Parkdirektor Riggers' and clematis 'Ascotiensis' in gay contrast.

Below left The single flowers of 'Scarlet Fire' glow amidst purple foliage.

Below right Aptly named 'Golden Showers' stands out against a brick wall.

brilliance of true scarlet, the single 'Soldier Boy' and 'Scarlet Fire', a splendid shrub that will also climb, are unbeatable.

The character of this garden is suited by the clear, bright colouring of many modern Floribunda roses, and gives a chance to use bushes of uniform height, closely planted, to form a multi-coloured carpet under weeping standards or as a surround to specimen shrubs; in other words, to use them as bedding plants. Specimen shrubs to choose from include the red roses 'Scarlet Fire', mentioned above; 'Will Scarlet', a semi-double Hybrid Musk with the bonus of orange-red hips; and the single-flowered, crimson scarlet 'Red Coat', which flowers continuously. Among the best yellow shrub roses are 'Golden Wings', 'Graham Thomas', 'Frühlingsgold' and 'Maigold'. There is no shortage of white shrub roses among old roses; then again there are the Hybrid Musks 'Moonlight' and 'Pax', the Rugosas, *R. rugosa* 'Alba' and 'Blanc Double de Coubert' and 'Nevada' (cream rather than white). The modern 'Iceberg', the most floriferous and continuous of all roses, will form a small shrub if pruned only lightly, and, if used in this way, is best planted in a group of three, 18 in/45 cm apart.

The use of roses as labour-saving bedding plants may seem un-attractively municipal and you may wonder what roses can do which cannot be done better by geraniums or petunias. But roses can, if chosen carefully, provide scent and individual beauty of flower as well as continuous bloom from late spring until autumn. They are not at their best massed solid with one variety to each bed, nor is the unplanned, multi-coloured effect that is seen in so many front gardens very satisfactory. However, if the pinks, apricots and purples are left out and the proportion of white roses to coloured is half and half, a pretty confetti of colour can be achieved.

Good Floribunda roses for this purpose, all between 2 ft/0·6 m and $2\frac{1}{2}$ ft/0·7 m in height, are 'Evelyn Fison' (brilliant scarlet, to be used sparingly), the Polyantha roses 'Gloria Mundi' and 'Miss Edith Cavell', 'Korona' (orange-scarlet, use sparingly) 'Lilli Marlene' (a good scarlet red), 'Orange Sensation', 'Paprika', 'Picasso' (red and white), 'Rob Roy' (crimson) and 'Rosemary Rose' (prone to mildew). Sadly, like almost all truly red roses, they lack scent. Of the yellows, 'Allgold', 'Korresia' and 'Yellow Cushion' are all the right height, but only 'Korresia' is strongly scented. It is difficult to find white roses to suit this scheme. 'Margaret Merrill' would be perfect if she were not a little too tall, and 'Iceberg' is definitely too tall, reaching 5 ft/1·5 m. 'Lady Romsey', however, has just about everything, including scent and a vigorous and tidy habit. Her white is suffused with soft creamy pink. Looking outside the Floribunda group, I would include the single Hybrid Tea rose 'White Wings', the beautifully behaved and always charming 'Little White Pet', and the slightly taller 'Yvonne Rabier' and 'Pearl Drift', the former for its scent and the latter for its pretty little flowers and glossy, dense foliage.

'Pearl Drift' is a procumbent rose, one of a group sometimes described as 'ground cover roses' since each plant is wider than it is tall and dense enough to be weed-smothering. They could be used instead of the Floribundas to make a more labour-saving, less formal scheme. Yellow is missing altogether from this group of roses, but a pretty tapestry could be made using the white 'Swany', 'Snow Carpet', 'Partridge', 'White Bells' and white 'Max Graf'. Colour would be added by 'Red Bells', 'Pink Bells', 'Pheasant', 'Red Max Graf', and 'Fairy Damsel' with deep red double flowers, and the newly introduced County Roses, available from Notcutts and bred to provide continuously flowering ground cover. They have not yet been around long enough to prove themselves, but 'Essex', 'Rutland', 'Sussex' and 'Surrey' (all pink), 'Suffolk' (scarlet) and 'Kent' (white) all show promise.

Both yellow and reds with any scarlet or orange pigmentation were latecomers to the rose-breeding scene, so thinking about this particular colour scheme has forced me into giving modern roses their due. I hope I may be absolved of old rose snobbery, but I have found it difficult to track down modern roses which combine those two valuable properties, scent and a graceful habit of growth.

My third garden will certainly depend for its effect mainly upon old roses, since only among them can the sumptuous opulence of flower shape and colour that is needed be found. This garden is inspired by the verse I quoted earlier from Vita Sackville-West's poem 'The Garden'. The atmosphere of Oriental splendour is evoked by the full-petalled purple-crimson velvet flowers of the Gallica roses 'Cardinal de Richelieu', 'Charles de Mills', 'Duc de Guiche' and 'Tuscany Superb'; the Centifolias 'Robert le Diable'

Scented roses for an opulent mood:

Above Brooding purple, grey and magenta mingle in the Old Velvet Moss rose 'William Lobb'.

Below left The lush, full-petalled blooms of the climber 'Blairii No. 2' are shaded from pale to rich pink.

Below right The rambler 'Veilchenblau' bears its lavender-purple flowers in huge trusses.

124

and 'Tour de Malakoff'; and the Hybrid Perpetuals 'Empereur du Maroc', 'Gloire de Ducher' and 'Reine des Violettes', the moss rose 'William Lobb', and the English Rose 'Othello', a rich crimson fading to purple and mauve.

Those roses which fade to subtle mixtures of soft violets, lilacs and greys are invaluable for weaving into the Persian carpet. They include the Gallicas 'Belle de Crécy', 'Jeanne Duval' and 'Nestor'. 'Magenta', 'Escapade' and 'Lilac Charm' are modern Floribunda roses with similar colouring. The soft depth of colour changes subtly as the flowers fade, giving varied intensity of tone within each shrub. They, and the striped roses form a good link between the darker reds and purples and the strong and pale pinks. Of the striped roses, the Bourbon 'Variegata di Bologna' is described by Peter Beales as reminscent of blackcurrant jam and semolina. Whether this combination appeals depends upon how you feel about semolina, but it is a beautiful rose and, although leggy as a shrub unless carefully pruned, it makes a beautiful climber. At Haddon Hall in Derbyshire it clothes a wall in the company of *Clematis* 'Mrs Cholmondley'. Other good striped roses include 'Camaieux' (Gallica), 'Tricolore de Flandres' which is similar to 'Camaieux' but a stronger shrub and therefore a better bet, the romantic and reliable 'Rosa Mundi' (Gallica), 'Commandant Beaurepaire' (Bourbon), 'Ferdinand Pichard' (Hybrid Perpetual) and 'Honorine de Brabant'.

Then there are the full, rich pink roses, their large, luscious blooms reminiscent of Edwardian ladies who wore their corsets with a purpose very different from that of the staid Victorians. Among these Merry Widow roses there are some excellent climbers: 'Madame Grégoire Staechelin' (happy on a north wall), 'Madame de Sancy de Parabère', climbing 'Souvenir de la Malmaison', 'Blairii No. 2' and the modern 'Aloha' and 'Constance Spry' are all winners. Pink shrub roses with an air of opulence could be chosen from among the Damasks, Portlands, Centifolias and Bourbons.

Perhaps the most luxurious and richest colours in roses, surpassing even the purples in this respect, are the deep, true reds of the climbers 'Etoile d'Hollande', 'Guinée' and climbing 'Château de Clos Vougeot'. They combine vibrant brilliance with an intensity of colour reminscent of freshly shed blood or the richest crimson velvet cloth. The same depth of red can be found in the shrubs 'Gruss an Teplitz', 'Wilhelm' (Hybrid Musk), 'Autumn Fire' and 'Fountain', and in Floribundas 'Dusky Maiden', 'Europeana' and 'Rob Roy'.

The somnolent opulence of these rich colours will need to be lightened here and there by contrasting shapes and colours. Climbers and ramblers which are in the same colour range but carry smaller, more delicate flowers in clusters include the purple 'Amadis' ('Crimson Boursault'), 'Bleu Magenta', 'Rose-Marie Viaud', 'Veilchenblau' and 'Violette'; 'Crimson Showers'; and the pink ramblers 'May Queen' and 'Kew Rambler'. For colour contrast among the climbers, I would plant yellows among the purples and crimsons, using, perhaps, 'Easleas Golden Rambler', 'Leverkusen', 'Gloire de Dijon' and 'Mermaid' on walls, and the ramblers 'Alister Stella Gray' and 'Goldfinch' for arch or arbour. The fading, slightly peachy yellows of these last two go particularly well with purple-red roses.

Touches of white here and there provide essential relief in a lush colour scheme, and suitable climbers include 'Paul's Lemon Pillar', 'Long John Silver', 'Sombreuil', 'Swan Lake' and 'White Cockade'. Near-white among the shrubs would be supplied by creamy 'Lady Romsey', 'Everest Double Fragrance' and 'Margaret Merrill', all Floribundas of medium to tall growth. (I will make suggestions for herbaceous plants for this scheme in my next chapter.)

This is not a colour scheme for gardens with brick walls and paving. It needs the quieter setting of grey or honey-coloured stone, and green lawns to prevent it becoming over-powering in its lushness. If water is included, a still pool with a large, single-flowered water-lily with its dinner-plate leaves would add to the mood of leisurely luxury. If there is moving water, it must gush rather than babble.

Each of these three rose gardens is planned to evoke a different mood. But of course there are as many moods as there are gardens, and it is for each gardener to choose his or her own, dictated either by the atmosphere that already exists in the garden or in its house, by the kind of roses the gardener loves best, or by the gardener's personal philosophy.

CHAPTER TWELVE

Complementary Planting

*Each portion now becomes a picture in itself, and every one is of such
a colouring that it best prepares the eye, in accordance with natural
law, for what is to follow. Standing for a few moments before the end-
most region of grey and blue, and saturating the eye to its utmost
capacity with these colours, it passes with extraordinary avidity to the
succeeding yellows. These intermingle in a pleasant harmony with the
reds and scarlets, blood-reds and clarets, and then lead again to yellows.
Now the eye has again become saturated, this time with the rich
colouring, and has therefore, by the law of complementary colour,
acquired a strong appetite for the greys and purples. These therefore
assume an appearance of brilliancy that they would not have had without
the preparation provided by their recently received complementary
colour.*

Gertrude Jekyll, *Colour Schemes for the Flower Garden*

If we agree with William Robinson that roses are not displayed
to the best advantage against a background of manure mixed
with straw, there is almost infinite scope for using other plants
behind, in front of, among and beneath the roses to enhance their
qualities of colour, form and scent. Shrubs, perennial plants and
bulbs can be chosen in colours and forms that will complement
the roses and with them compose a pleasing picture. Additional
planting in the rose garden provides an opportunity, too, to
extend the period of flowering to the spring and beyond the rose
season into autumn.

I have already touched upon the importance of a dense, sober
background to the roses, a mature yew hedge being the ideal for
all roses except those of the darkest reds and purples. Their heavy
colours tend to disappear against a dark background; they show
better against the fresh green of beech or hornbeam. Copper or
purple foliage, either growing free or clipped into a hedge, also
makes a background which enhances the richness of the stronger
reds and sets off roses of paler colouring. Roses in the buff-yellow
to soft apricot colour range are also enhanced by purple foliage,
and it can be used too to separate them from the strong pinks
and reds. The claret vine, *Vitis vinifera* 'purpurea', trained on a
wall, trellis or high fence, makes a good background to roses,

128

A border in the Rose Garden at Sissinghurst in late June.

and looks superb with a scarlet climber, such as 'Soldier Boy', or a buff one, such as 'Gloire de Dijon'. In an informal setting, the purple hazel (*Corylus maxima* 'Purpurea') *Cotinus coggyria* 'Foliis Purpureis', *Berberis thunbergii* 'Atropurpurea' and *Prunus × cistena*, as free-growing, untrimmed shrubs, make a good background to shrub roses.

For background planting and interspersed among the roses, shrubs with dense foliage and firm shape are needed to give the structure that is lacking in the loose, open habit of growth of most roses. If these shrubs are also to be evergreen, and to flower either before or after the summer season of the roses, then the choice is limited. Earliest to flower and a sight for sore eyes throughout mild winters is *Viburnum tinus*. April brings the divine scent of *Osmanthus delavayi, Osmanthus × burkwoodii* (*Osmarea × burkwoodii*), and *Viburnum burkwoodii*, all with white flowers and good evergreen foliage.

In late spring, *Choisya ternata*, one of the very best of evergreen shrubs, bears its deliciously fragrant flowers, and two useful compact forms of *Prunus laurocerasus*, 'Otto Luyken' and 'Zabeliana', produce tidy spikes of white flowers. Where there is space, other good spring-flowering shrubs can be added, and their foliage will form a green backdrop to the roses when their flowering season is over. Trained against a wall, varieties of *Chaenomeles speciosa* (japonica) were flowering in my garden in Gloucestershire as early as mid-February in 1988, and continued through April. It is a useful shrub to hide the legs of climbing roses to a height of 6 ft/1·8 m or so. *Viburnum × carlcephalum* and *V. juddii* would be included for their heavenly scent, *V. plicatum* 'Mariesii' for its beautiful, tiered habit of growth, and as many tree peonies as there is space for, since, as well as spectacularly beautiful flowers they carry foliage of great distinction.

The bare ground beneath the rose bushes provides a double opportunity: low herbaceous plants can be inter-planted with spring bulbs. For use as carpeting plants there are ajugas, prostrate campanulas, *Omphalodes cappadocica, Brunnera macrophylla, Lamium maculatum*, pulmonaria and violas. Bulbs will look their best if not more than two kinds, or two colours of the same kind, are planted together in interlocking drifts: snowdrops with aconites for the very earliest flowering, or cream and blue species crocuses or chionodoxa with dwarf narcissi. To flower a little later, in formal rose beds, *Tulipa kaufmanniana*, with their broad, striped leaves would be effective. An alternative would be to plant taller herbaceous plants such as *Dicentra spectabilis* (particularly the white one) between the roses, to usher in their flowering season.

The choice of shrubs to follow the roses in their flowering is harder. Hydrangeas are a possibility, but the mop-heads should be avoided among those roses which have a second flush of bloom in early autumn, such as the Hybrid Musks and some of the Bourbons. *Hydrangea sargentiana* and *H. villosa*, however, would be good in the back row, with their large leaves and lace-cap flower heads of dusky mauve. Also in the back row, escallonias would provide colour late in the season, and have the bonus of evergreen leaves, as do the flowering privets, *Ligustrum japonicum*, *L. lucidum* and the distinguished *L. quihoui*. These tall graceful shrubs are much neglected. I suppose the name 'privet' puts people off. A smaller shrub, up to 5 ft/1·5 m, full of grace and flowering from late mid-summer into autumn, is *Abelia × grandiflora*. Not entirely hardy, it needs a sheltered position. In late summer many of the blue-flowered shrubs come into their own and associate well with the yellow, apricot and salmon shades of Hybrid Musk roses, coinciding with their second flush of flowering. Caryopteris, Perovskia, *Buddleia* 'Lochinch' and *B.* 'Nanho Blue' all have the added charm of grey foliage.

There are two herbaceous plants that are particularly useful to follow on after the roses: *Phlox paniculata* and *Anemone hybrida*. Both make their attractive foliage unobtrusively while the roses are giving their display, neither needs staking, and the phlox will be at their best in late summer, the Japanese anemones in late summer and early autumn.

The foreground is equally important. A uniform edging to rose beds, whether formal or informal, helps to pull the whole scheme together, and can be useful in hiding the legs of the roses which are, on the whole, not an attribute to which one would wish to draw attention. The true green of box, midway between blue and yellow, is the perfect, restful foil to every other colour, and is a traditional edging plant in formal rose gardens. It is slow growing, but in the long run that is an advantage as it can be kept neat and tidy with just an annual haircut.

Where grey foliage is wanted, particularly in order to make a visual break between pink and crimson roses and brick paths or walls, the more compact forms of lavender are useful. The soft blue-purple of lavender goes well with roses of all colours. If it seems to have become rather a cliché, pink or white lavenders are a chic alternative, though they are less reliably hardy. *L. spica* 'Loddon Pink' is about 18 in/0·4 m high, and *L. spica* 'Nana Alba' is a real dwarf at 9 in/22 cm. An alternative to lavender, producing the same effect of grey leaves and mauve flowers over a long period, is catmint (*Nepeta mussenii* or *N. × fassennii*). *Santolina chamaecyparissus* 'Nana' makes a tidy silvery-grey edging as long as its mustard-yellow button flowers, which are held erect in a rather ungainly fashion on thin but stiff stalks, are removed.

Another unusual evergreen plant for dwarf hedging is *Teucrium chamaedrys* (germander). Rosemary, too, can be clipped into a hedge of rather larger dimensions. Where a low hedge of red-purple is wanted. *Berberis thunbergii* 'Atropurpurea Nana' can be used; it looks very effective in part of the extensive rose gardens at Castle Howard.

In a rose garden of smaller scale, edgings can be useful as well as ornamental. Chives and parsley are both said to ward off greenfly, so are particularly appropriate, and Alpine strawberries are pretty used either as edging or as ground cover under roses. Other possibilities are golden marjoram, thrift, or one of the taller thymes.

In very informal schemes, combined diversity and unity can be achieved by fronting rose borders with mixed plants of similar foliage colour. Thus, where grey is wanted in a fairly large-scale planting, *Senecio* 'Sunshine', *Dorycnium hirsutum*, *Santolina neapolitana* (with more feathery, white-silver leaves and of a looser, more graceful habit than *S. chamaecyparissus*), *Ballota pseudodictamnus*, *Hebe pinguifolia* 'Pagei', lavenders and sage (*Salvia officinalis*) can all be used, spilling on to a paved terrace or path or draping a low wall. The purple sage, *Salvia officinalis* 'Purpurascens' bridges the categories of grey and purple foliage, its mat, dusky purple leaves being overlaid with a grey haze. *Berberis thunbergii* 'Atropurpurea Nana' makes a shrub of about 2 ft × 2 ft/60 cm × 60 cm and needs planting in groups of three or more. Apart from these two shrubs, one has to look to herbaceous perennials for low-growing plants with purple foliage, to *Ajuga*

At Lytes Carey, Somerset, roses are complemented by nepeta, *Alchemilla mollis* and *Papaver orientalis* backed by purple foliage.

reptans 'Atropurpurea' which will creep too far if you allow it to, *Heuchera* 'Palace Purple', *Saxifraga fortunei* 'Wada', and *Viola labradorica* which seeds itself happily around but is easy to pull out where it is not wanted.

Edgings, forming bays and inlets at the front of a border, can be made with pinks, one of the classic companions to roses; *Stachys olympica*; any of the grey-leaved helianthemums; or *Veronica incana*. (For a full list of plants see Appendix B.)

Plants to grow through and among the roses will be mainly herbaceous; it is only too easy to be seduced into thinking in terms of their flowers to the exclusion of other important considerations, such as the colour and form of their leaves when not in flower, and the form of the plant when flowering. Monotony in the rose garden can be avoided if special attention is paid to the vertical line. Plants with spikey leaves are invaluable for this purpose, as are flowers which are held along upright stems. Irises, hemerocallis, crocosmia, *Libertia formosa*, *Sisyrinchium striatum*, phormiums and yuccas all have bold, sword-like or strap-shaped leaves which enable them to play an important role when they are not in flower.

Plants with bold, broad leaves provide another antidote to the formlessness of rose bushes, particularly for foreground planting, giving the eye something solid to focus on amidst a confusion of flowers. The hostas, bergenias, crambes, hellebores and verbascums are stars in this respect, and there are many more. I also consider *Alchemilla mollis* to be a star, although it is so generous with its seedlings that it risks becoming a nuisance. There is no other leaf colour quite like its soft, pale green and this, together with its foaming lime flowers and the round, delicately frilled leaves which hold raindrops like diamonds on a jade saucer make it the perfect companion to bright pink roses.

Those plants which bear tall flower spikes are of great value among roses. Acanthus, delphiniums, foxgloves, eremurus, sisyrinchium, the tall campanulas, some lilies, salvias, verbascums and veronicas come into this category and flower with the roses.

The colour relationship of these and any other flowers to be used with the roses needs to be considered carefully. There is really no short cut to reaching this understanding and time spent studying diagrams of the spectral wheel and charts which demonstrate hues, tints, shades and tones will pay dividends. (You will find such diagrammatic analysis of colour in Penelope Hobhouse's book, in Graham Stuart Thomas's *The Art of Planting* and, to illustrate Gertrude Jekyll's approach, in *Gardens of a Golden Afternoon* by Jane Brown.)

It is a simple matter to make a colour wheel by dividing a circle into segments and colouring the segments in the order in which colours appear in the rainbow. Leaving out indigo, you end up with six segments to the circle, with green opposite red, blue opposite orange and violet opposite yellow. These pairs are important: they are 'complementary' colours, and provide the strongest possible contrasts, the colours in each pair intensifying each other and giving the greatest possible stimulation to the eye. Satisfying contrasts can also be made by pairing a colour with one of the neighbours of its opposite, for example, blue with yellow, or green with orange. These contrasts work equally well using the pure colours, their tints (paling towards white), shades (darkening towards black) or tones (the pure colour subdued towards grey).

Other important principles, summarised briefly, are:

- 'Warm' colours (red and orange and their neighbours, red-violet and orange-yellow) are exciting to the eye and appear to advance.

- 'Cool' colours (blue and green, blue-violet and green-yellow) are reposeful and appear to recede.

- A pure colour, plus its paler tint, plus white is always harmonious.

- Adjacent colours used together are usually harmonious, for example, red and violet, or orange and yellow.

- Dark tones of colour give weight and stability to a scheme.

When working out a colour scheme, it is important to achieve a balance between harmony and contrast. A garden which concentrates exclusively on harmony and repose may appear a little monotonous: a garden full of contrasts can be hectic and tiring.

To give an idea of possible colour combinations, I will suggest two imaginary examples, one for a 'cool' colour scheme, and one for a 'warm' one.

In the cool rose garden, the roses will be predominantly in those shades of pink which have a hint of blue in them. To the pinks can be added ice-maiden white, pale blush and, for contrasting stronger colour, used sparingly, a few of the softer purples and striped roses.

Complementary planting will include plenty of blues. The shades that will flatter these roses best are the softer blues, which share with pink roses a hint of lavender in their make-up. Such shades can be found among the delphiniums. Other plants with tall spikes of flowers, to plant at the back of the rose border, and between shrub roses, include *Campanula lactiflora*, aptly named for its great trusses of closely set, milky blue bells, and *Campanula persicifolia*, with its bells set further apart all the way up the stems. Dwarf, creeping campanulas and *Viola cornuta* which will find its way up the legs of a rose bush as well as forming a low mat, are useful edging plants and, among those of intermediate size, *Geranium* 'Johnson's Blue' is a wonderfully intense colour and forms a shapely mound. A little later, overlapping with the roses, but taking the flowering season into late summer, come the balloon-flowers of *Platycodon grandiflorum* and the grey-blue bells of codonopsis.

Shades of lavender deepening into purple will link these blues to the pinks of the roses, *Lavandula spica* 'Hidcote' or 'Munstead Dwarf' making compact clumps of violet-purple, and traditional English Lavender forming a larger, looser plant with paler flower spikes. Catmint is invaluable for its long flowering period. In the background, *Buddleia alternifolia* 'argentea' makes a gracefully arching mound some 9 × 6 ft/2·7 × 1·8 m or more wide, with silvery willow-like leaves and wands smothered in tiny lavender flowers. This shrub can be trained as a standard and is an excellent, smaller alternative for the rather over-used weeping silver pear.

The scheme would also benefit from plants with flowers or paler or darker pinks than the roses, with contrasting forms. The common foxglove, *Digitalis purpurea*, and its white form are perfect for this purpose, and can be seen at Mottisfont Abbey, at Helmingham Hall and in other successful rose gardens. There are also pink forms of delphinium, *Campanula lactiflora* and verbascum for spikes, *Geranium endressii*, *G. macrorrhizum* and 'Russell Prichard' for mounds, and *Armeria maritima*, dianthus,

Above left A cool colour scheme of pure yellow with paler yellows and white added, and foliage of greens and greys. Parc de Belvédère, Louhm, Belgium.

Above right Strong, warm colours: golden yellow *R. ecae* 'Helen Knight' and tawny orange wallflowers, at Sissinghurst.

Bottom left 'Easlea's Golden Rambler', on the cool side of yellow, cooled further by the mauve-blue clematis 'Ascotiensis'.

Bottom right Warm reds and pinks at Arley Hall, harmoniously cooled by the mauve nepeta.

136

helianthemums, and *Gypsophila paniculata* 'Rosy Veil' for edging.

Any restrained colour scheme is improved by occasional splashes of a contrasting colour, used with caution, and in this case the pinks and purples could be enlivened with a brushstroke here and there of one of the softer shades of yellow by adding roses of this colouring, the dramatic spires of *Verbascum bombyciferum*, *Asphodeline lutea* or *Eremurus bungei*, the flat plates of *Achillea* 'Moonshine', the tidy spikes of *Sisyrinchium striatum*, the soft yellow foxglove, *Digitalis grandiflora* (*D. ambigua*) (very effective at Mottisfont) and, at the feet of the roses, *Alchemilla mollis* or *Oenothera missouriensis*, the low-growing evening primrose.

White is an essential ingredient, to highlight other colours, and many of the plants I have already mentioned have white forms. There will certainly be some white roses, and other plants with white flowers should be chosen for their contrasting form: the clouds of tiny white stars of *Gypsophila paniculata* 'Bristol Fairy' or *Crambe cordifolia*, *Libertia formosa* with its sword-shaped leaves, astrantia's little greenish-pink pin-cushions, the creamy plumes of *Aruncus sylvester*, or *Dicentra spectabilis* 'Alba', its arching stems hung with white lockets, would all serve the purpose well. Thus, the colour scheme consists of variations on the main colour, pink, provided by its spectral neighbour mauve, shading into soft lavender blues; strength is added by stronger, darker shades of violet and purple-pink, contrast by the yellows, and sparkling light by the essential white.

The same basic recipe can be applied to the warm colour scheme, which will be based on roses of true red, crimson and purple-crimson colouring. Up to one-third of the roses would be striped, white, and dusky pink, to relieve an overall effect which might otherwise be too heavy and sombre. But the desired effect is one of great richness, so that additional planting would include in good measure the strong violets that were used only sparingly in the cool scheme. I would add the startling magenta of *Geranium psilostemon*.

The complementary contrast of scarlet-reds with the bright green foliage of, say, a beech hedge, makes a strong impact but may be too startling and restless, whereas the purple hues of coppery foliage will harmonise with strong red and take the harshness out of it. For small areas of contrast in a bold scheme, acid yellow-green, the directly complementary colour to red-violet, provides the required astringent contrast to richly sumptuous crimsons and purples. This sharpness can be provided by the leaves of *Sambucus racemosa* 'Plumosa Aurea', or *Lonicera nitida* 'Baggesen's Gold', *Philadelphus coronarius* 'Aureus' or *Catalpa bignonioides* 'Aurea', the latter pruned hard to keep it to shrub dimensions and to increase the size of its dramatic leaves. To keep the greenish tinge to their yellow foliage, these shrubs need some shade from the midday sun, and the leaves of the philadelphus will scorch at the edges if grown in full sun. No such strictures apply to *Euphorbia characias wulfenii*, *E. polychroma* (*E. epithymoides*), *E. palustris* and *E. myrsinites*.

Euphorbia griffithii 'Fireglow' has brick-orange flower-heads, always hard to place, but would look good with the single shrub rose 'Scarlet Fire' and the soft yellow of *Achillea* 'Moonshine'. The quieter, more buttery yellows suggested for the cool colour scheme are equally useful to add cooler, contrasting splashes to the hot scheme. The hot reds and strong purples can be separated and softened with grey foliage and with lavender flowers: *Geranium renardii*, *Salvia haematodes* and the spectacular, tall *Salvia sclarea turkestanica* with its large lilac-pink and white bracts are all first-class plants for this purpose. The green-white flowers of *Astrantia major*, *Heuchera* 'Greenfinch' and *Tiarella cordifolia*, or the very pale lilac flowers of *Hosta crispula*, *H. fortunei* or *H. sieboldiana* will have a softer, more harmonious effect than pure white and, in the front row, the smaller dicentras are ideal, with their elegantly fine-cut glaucous leaves, some slightly tinged with purple, and their little sprays of soft pink-purple locket flowers.

Gardens to visit for inspiration, where the colour schemes have been planned with care, include Crathes Castle, Hidcote, Powis Castle, Tintinhull, and many other National Trust gardens and, among privately owned gardens, the Brewhouse in Kent, Chilcombe House (described in Part III), Wyken Hall in Suffolk, Brook Cottage, Oxfordshire and Greatham Mill, Hampshire.

In the wild garden, too, the right companion plants can transform a collection of shrub and species roses into a garden or a romantic landscape. The same sober background is desirable here as in the formal rose garden. In the wild garden it will be a background of woodland, hedgerow or densely planted shrubs whose flowering season is over before the roses bloom, or else is yet to come. When roses are dotted about in grass, with no additional shrub planting, an opportunity is lost. After the spring flowering of small bulbs in generous drifts, followed by daffodils and bluebells, the effect will be spotty and unnatural unless the roses can be linked into clumps, thickets or belts by interplanting with other, more solid shrubs. Around and between the clumps, herbaceous plants can be planted in the kind of groups that might form naturally at the base of a hedgerow, or on the perimeter of a wood. Such groups sometimes develop with no help from the gardener. With luck, cow parsley, foxgloves, meadow cranesbill, moon daisies, campions and mallows will arrive without encouragement. Unfortunately, so will nettles, docks and thistles, and these will need to be eradicated to give more decorative species a chance.

Natural colonisers can be supplemented by those herbaceous plants that are robust enough to look after themselves. William Robinson in *The Wild Garden* (first published in 1870) lists many, including delphiniums and others which cannot really be trusted to thrive unaided. But those capable of holding their own and increasing their territory over the years include peonies, lupins, *Aruncus sylvester*, *Foeniculum vulgare* (particularly good in its purple-leaved form), *Crambe cordifolia*, *Campanula lactiflora*, *Geranium macrorrhizum* and *Papaver orientalis*, which all flower with the roses. Others which follow the roses in flower, with good foliage to give structure to the planting scheme, are acanthus, Japanese anemones and crocosmia.

Climbing and rambler roses on walls, arches and arbours can also benefit from the companionship of other plants. Other climbing plants can be chosen either for the colour of their flowers or leaves, to complement the roses, or for the size and shape of their leaves to give a bold background to the roses. On walls, self-clinging climbers are the most trouble-free and will hug the wall neatly without interfering with the roses.

Plants which climb by twining tendrils will, if they are vigorous species, strangle the roses, but can look very fine alternating with the roses on a pergola or tunnel, to provide contrasting leaf form and colour. A structure of sufficient size and robust construction provides an opportunity to use some of the ornamental vines which are too vigorous for a small porch or a dainty wire arch.

Above Hot, strong colours, contrasting with a cool, green background: roses with *Foeniculum vulgare*.

Below A gentler scheme, the fennel's bright yellow softened by the peachy tones of the roses, and further cooled by pale blue linum.

Vitis coignetiae has huge, handsome leaves up to 10 in/25 cm long and wide, and brilliant crimson autumn colouring. Vines that produce grapes which ripen in Britain and can be used for wine-making include *Vitis vinifera* 'Purpurea' with plum-coloured leaves darkening in autumn to a rich purple, and the perfect background to ramblers with the colour of 'Goldfinch' or 'Alister Stella Gray', and *V. vinifera* 'Incana', which has pale, grey-green leaves covered in fine white down, which look good with red, crimson and purple roses. These two vines are also effective planted together. As handsome as *Vitis coignetiae* and with leaves almost as large, is *Actinidia chinensis*. Its fruits are Chinese gooseberries or kiwi fruit and will ripen in a warm summer.

Clematis is the classic climbing companion to the rose, but *C. montana* and its varieties should be avoided as it will choke most roses to death after a few years. Many of the clematis species, with their delicate flowers are ideal for planting with those roses which have a comparatively short flowering season. They are not vigorous enough to provide unwelcome competition, their young foliage will clothe the bare legs of the roses, and they will flower either before or after the roses get under way. *Clematis alpina* and *C. macropetala* flower in spring, *C. orientalis*, *C. texensis* and *C. viticella* through the summer till early autumn. There is also a wide choice of large-flowered clematis hybrids to flower with and after the roses, in a range of colours from white and lavender-pink through purple-reds and violets to pale or deep blues.

Several other climbers merit consideration for use with roses: jasmine and the honeysuckles on arches and arbours will mingle their scent with that of the roses or provide scent among roses which lack it. *Solanum jasminoides* 'Album' (not always hardy) is semi-evergreen, fast-growing and has white flowers with yellow centres held in graceful, loose clusters from mid-summer to late autumn, and *Solanum crispum* 'Glasnevin' has flowers like the potato plant in a rich shade of violet blue to complement yellow roses.

It is tempting to forget that the roses are intended to be the stars of the show, that the other plants used are not rivals for stardom but humble members of the chorus. A few kinds boldly grouped and carefully chosen for their form, texture and colour to precede, accompany or follow the roses in their flowering will help the roses to give an unforgettable performance.

PART THREE

---❁---

Some Outstanding Rose Gardens

EAST END FARM, PITNEY, SOMERSET

The garden at East End Farm is an example of how much can be achieved in a relatively small space, on a site of unpromising proportions. There is a small, paved garden at the front of the house and behind it an area not much larger than the back gardens of many terraced houses. Some 239 sq yds/200 sq m of this space is taken up by barns and outbuildings.

When Mrs Wray came to the low, L-shaped, seventeenth-century stone farmhouse in 1946 the only assets were these outbuildings and the mellow stone walls enclosing the farmyard that was to become her garden. They provided shelter for plants and complete privacy for the occupants. In order to get the new garden off to a good start, she brought a number of favourite roses with her.

Now, after some forty years of loving, thoughtful gardening, to enter this garden at any time of year is to enter a world of intimate, orderly tranquillity. A pleasurable sense of order is provided by the simple symmetry of the layout, by the well-kept lawns and by the tidy, flat umbrella shapes of the avenue of *Malus × lemoinei* that frame the central walk. These trees are an inspired choice: in April their prolific cerise blossom is spectacular, and later their sculptured shape and deep purple foliage supply exactly the right sober foil for the roses.

One of the things that make this garden so satisfying is its firm sense of direction. No attempt has been made to disguise the long, narrow, rectangular space. On the contrary, it is turned to advantage by the placing of a long, central walk leading, in the shade of the malus avenue, along a vista flanked by borders of roses at eye and nose level, richly underplanted with perennials in cottage garden style. Half way along the walk a cross-path is punctuated by a simple stone bowl set in a paved square edged with thyme, and at the end of the vista there is a stone seat, also set in thyme and framed by a screen of roses, 'Mrs F. W. Flight', 'Félicité et Perpétue', 'Fantin-Latour', 'Veilchenblau' and 'Paul's Himalayan Musk'. The seat invites you to rest and look back towards the house along borders which include, among the many old roses, 'Président de Sèze', 'Jenny Duval', 'Honorine de Bra-

144

Old roses frame an intimate vista to the low stone bird-bath set in a carpet of thyme.

bant', 'Goldfinch', 'Belle de Crécy', and mossy 'William Lobb'.

Behind the stone seat there is an open area of lawn, bounded to the south by two large and handsome stone barns, and to the east and west by walls. The end of the garden seems to have been reached and you prepare to return to the house by one of the side, rose-bordered walks. But there is a further, almost secret garden beyond the two great barns. A path flanked with raised rock beds runs between the barns, planted with Burnet roses, saxifrages, dianthus, hardy cyclamen and aquilegia. It leads through a timber fence on to a lawn completely enclosed by walls, with raised beds of roses, a gallery of stout timber posts supporting climbing roses on the west side, and a little terrace paved with stone on edge with a central sundial surrounded with mature and gnarled rosemary bushes on the east. Presiding over this quiet enclosure is a charming bronze figure of a young boy: known as the Rose Shepherd, he stands on a stone column above a still pool.

There are many other things to notice at East End Farm: an unruly 'Kiftsgate' rose outgrowing its stout metal support, roses growing in crab apple trees, honeysuckles and clematis varieties amongst the roses on walls and trees. And, although the roses are all-important, there are many other shrubs, perennials and bulbs to make the garden special at all times.

145

HADDON HALL, BAKEWELL, DERBYSHIRE

By great good luck the eighteenth-century passion for the improvement of houses and their grounds bypassed Haddon Hall. The Dukes of Rutland, who had acquired the Hall by the marriage of Sir John Manners to Dorothy Vernon in the sixteenth century, preferred to live at Belvoir Castle in Lincolnshire. Haddon Hall remained uninhabited and its house and gardens neglected from the beginning of the eighteenth century until early in this century when the ninth Duke set about a meticulous restoration of the house to the perfect example of a medieval hall that we see today.

It is probable that the layout of the gardens, like the structure of the house, remained unaltered after 1641 when John Manners succeeded to the Earldom of Rutland and, having completed his alterations to the Long Gallery at Haddon, transferred his energies to Belvoir. Thus the splendid series of terraces embracing the east and south fronts of the Hall and descending in giant steps to the great loop in the River Wye beneath the Hall appear to us today much as they did to Dorothy Vernon whose family had already lived there for four hundred years when she inherited the property in 1567.

During the nineteenth century the uninhabited Hall and its overgrown gardens became famous as a romantic example of the picturesque and it was much visited by artists, poets and sightseers including Queen Victoria and Prince Albert. The restoration of the gardens was carried out in the 1920s, respecting the ancient layout of the terraces, but softening their contours with a profusion of roses. Many of the roses at Haddon date from this period and have become rare today.

The gardens at Haddon are hidden from the visitor at first. You arrive, through a gateway in the North West Tower, into the Lower Courtyard which is enclosed on all sides by stone walls, towers and bays, its floor paved in the same weathered stone of grey and warm buff. The paving on the ground is uninterrupted except for a little herb knot in one corner, but the walls give promises of pleasures to come. They are covered in roses: 'Albertine', 'Allen Chandler', 'Lady Waterlow', 'Mme Caroline Testout', 'Le Rêve', and 'Zéphirine Drouhin', giving an uninhibited display

Plan and section showing the layout of the terraces at Haddon Hall.

146

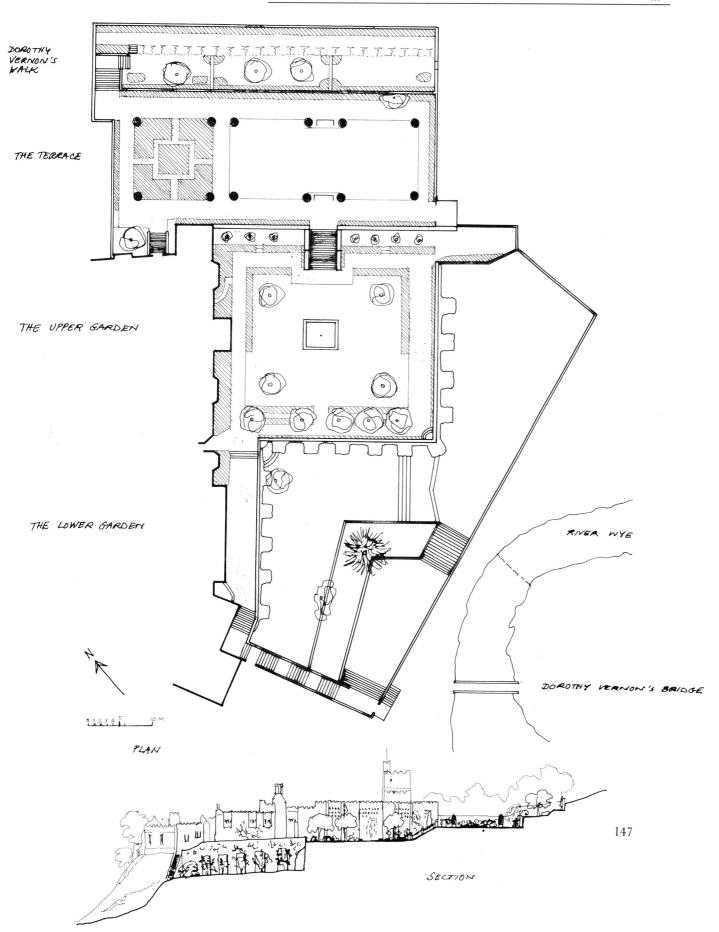

DOROTHY VERNON'S WALK

THE TERRACE

THE UPPER GARDEN

THE LOWER GARDEN

RIVER WYE

DOROTHY VERNON'S BRIDGE

N

0 1 2 3 4 5   10 M

PLAN

SECTION

147

of colour which will be repeated spectacularly elsewhere in the gardens.

After absorbing the atmosphere within the panelled rooms of the Hall, one of grandeur tempered with domesticity, you open a door in the gloom of a small panelled ante-room and find yourself at the top of Dorothy Vernon's steps, traditionally the route by which she crept out to elope with Sir John Manners. If you go to Haddon on a rainy day, your first impression on opening this door will be of an elusive yet pervasive, spicy scent. It is the scent of the leaves of *Rosa primula*, the Incense Rose which, after rain, fills the air over a considerable distance. Simultaneously, you receive such an impression of light and colour from the rose beds below you that you have to look again at the leaden sky to see whether the sun has suddenly come out.

The outer beds of the simple rectangular design are planted with blocks of Hybrid Tea roses: 'Amatsu Otome', the deep crimson 'Madame Louis Laperrière', salmon 'Mischief', yellow

A view from the top terrace. The balustraded steps are flanked by the Alba rose 'Celestial'.

148

'King's Ransom', 'Alec's Red' and pink 'Wendy Cussons'. The central bed is planted with 'Ballerina', lavender and the striped 'Honorine de Brabant', and the paths into this little rose garden are flanked by 'Celsiana' and 'Rosa Mundi'. The beds are edged with grey-leaved helianthemums and under-planted with blue and purple violas. Behind the rose beds stretches the massive wall that retains the topmost terrace for a length of some 65 yd/60 m. At its foot is a herbaceous border, and the whole wall is covered with roses, including the fragrant, rich red 'Souvenir de Claudius Denoyel', 'Shot Silk', 'Madame Edouard Herriot', 'Le Rêve', 'Excelsa', 'Madame Grégoire Staechelin' and 'Minnehaha'. At the top of the wall are beds of 'Frensham', 'Cornelia' and 'Morgensonne', and still higher are more climbing roses on the wall bounding the top terrace.

From the main terrace you can look over the handsome, stone, seventeenth-century balustrade to the Upper Garden below. It was decorated with parterres at the time that it was made, laid out to be viewed from the windows of the Long Gallery, and it is now given over chiefly to roses. You descend by a long and broad flight of steps, their balustraded sides smothered with 'Albertine'. The central lawn has a simple stone pool with a fountain, and *Malus* 'Golden Hornet' at each of its four corners. In front of you at either side as you descend the steps are standard 'Ballerina' underplanted with 'Nypels Perfection', and the beds bordering the lawn are given over to Floribunda roses in scarlet, pink and yellow. As everywhere at Haddon, the walls are smothered in roses, mixed with carefully chosen clematis varieties. Among those roses seldom seen today are 'Alida Lovett', 'Surpassing Beauty of Woolverstone', 'General MacArthur', 'Champney's Pink Cluster', 'Christine' and 'Colonel Poole'. From the little platform in the south east corner of this garden you can look down on to the river, where it forms a great loop towards the Hall. Below you are the massive buttresses supporting the Upper Garden, with roses rambling over them and self-sown aubrieta and campanula colonising crevices in the stone structure.

Nowhere at Haddon are the colour schemes contrived. The roses grow in a kaleidoscopic confusion of reds, pinks, apricots and yellows tumbling from one level to the next, and the gay and high-spirited scene is contained and anchored by the massive solidity of four-hundred-year-old stone.

DUXFORD MILL, DUXFORD, CAMBRIDGESHIRE

Robert Lea at Duxford Mill shares with Humphrey Brooke at Lime Kiln (see pages 153–4) a belief in minimal pruning. In all other respects his garden is completely different.

Robert Lea bought the derelict Mill with thirteen acres of land in 1947 and, after restoring the house, set about making a garden on five acres of unpromisingly bleak and windswept chalk overlaid with river silt. Shelter was provided by surrounding the site with fast-growing Leyland cypress interspersed with yews, with a view to the long term. The site is bounded by the River Cam; its greatest asset is the mill stream which curves through the centre of the garden providing, together with a wide expanse of lawn each side of it, a feeling of spaciousness. A large weeping willow marks the curve of the stream, and birch groves and other groups of flowering trees are planted at strategic points, framing the main vista to a classical temple on the north boundary, and a secondary vista to a large statue of two angels on the east side of the garden.

After struggling for some years with a labour-intensive 65 yd/60 m herbaceous border in front of the west-facing belt of Leyland cypress, Robert Lea decided that the best way to have colour in the garden over a long period and with a minimum of work would be to grow roses. The idea of roses being labour-saving will still seem eccentric today to anyone who grows Floribunda and Hybrid Tea roses in the traditional way, pruning, feeding, weeding and spraying at the appropriate times.

But at Duxford Mill you will see a very successful departure from this tradition. The roses, mostly Floribundas, but some Hybrid Teas as well, are planted in borders 3 yd/3 m wide, in four rows, the very vigorous varieties at the back, then two rows of medium growers and a row of shorter roses in front. Closer spacing than is usually seen is important, both for the dense and luxuriant effect when the roses are in flower, and to deter weed growth. Pruning consists only of the removal of dead or frosted wood and, in the autumn, the shortening of very tall shoots to prevent wind-rock. Weeding is carried out by an application of weedkiller in the spring, feeding by one application of fertiliser, followed later in the season by a foliar feed. Spraying against

TO STREAM-SIDE
WALK AND WILD-
FOWL ENCLOSURE

ENTRANCES
TO GARDEN

MILL POND

STATUE

RIVER

GREEK
TEMPLE

N

0 5 10
METERS

a ROSE BEDS
b SHRUB BEDS
c PLANTS GROWN FOR CUT FLOWERS

Plan showing the layout of the garden at Duxford Mill.

fungus and greenfly is carried out approximately once every three weeks during the summer, and the roses are watered during dry spells, but this would be necessary for most plants in such exceptionally free-draining conditions.

To achieve the best results, it is important to use roses of strong and healthy constitution, and to choose those that flower prolifically and over a long period. In order to discover which roses fulfil these criteria, Robert Lea has kept records, charting the number of flowers on each plant and the length of flowering

151

season over several years. For comparison, he also charted shrubby potentillas (generally considered to flower over a very long period), some clematis varieties and various bedding plants. Most of the roses out-performed the potentillas easily; among the clematis varieties, 'Mrs Cholmondley' came close to the average floribunda rose but nowhere near the top scorers; and bedding plants, especially petunias, were out in front doing as well as, but not better than, the best of the roses.

In the league table, the highest scorer is good old 'Iceberg', with 'Patricia McAlpine', a new rose bred by Robert Lea, only one point behind and, again one point behind, 'Amber Queen', followed by 'Marlena', 'Dorothy Wheatcroft', 'Matangi' and two more of Mr Lea's roses, not yet formally named. Others that did well were 'Allgold', 'Eye Paint', 'Intrigue' and 'Scarlet O'Hara'. It is good to see that the lovely white Hybrid Perpetual rose, 'Frau Karl Druschki' does nearly as well as those mentioned above. Sadly, few of the roses that provide such abundance and continuity of flower have much scent.

There is no colour planning here, yet the juxtapositions never seem to jar, and the overall effect is rich and lively against the calm setting of still water and immaculate lawn.

The main, multi-coloured rose border seen across the mill pond.

152

LIME KILN ROSARIUM, CLAYDON, SUFFOLK

At Lime Kiln the roses seem to possess the place completely. They seem more permanent than the house which is almost completely hidden beneath them. This impression is reinforced by seeing, in the jungle below the garden, the huge rose which is said to be a seedling that has reverted to a type known from fossils to have grown between 350,000 and 500,000 B C.

The fact that the roses seem so completely settled and at home is all the more surprising considering the unpromising site at Lime Kiln. Although the garden is well sheltered on all sides by belts of trees, the soil is solid chalk. Humphrey Brooke's methods of cultivation will be of interest to anyone who gardens on chalk: generous planting holes are cut and, once planted, the roses are left to fend for themselves. Feeding and watering are avoided, as this would draw the vulnerable young roots towards the surface. The objective is to encourage the roses to root deep into the chalk where they will find what nourishment and moisture is available.

A corner of the paved garden.

The system clearly works. It is also possible that Mr Brooke's 'no pruning' policy has contributed to the health and vigour of the plants. Certainly the rose bushes grow to larger sizes than are usually seen and flower in greater profusion. There is a spectacular plant of 'Perle d'Or' here, famous among rose enthusiasts, which is more than double its 'normal' height and breadth.

The policy of *laisser faire* is extended to the underplanting beneath the roses, reinforcing the impression of generous profusion. Although there is no pruning of the roses, apart from the removal of dead wood when necessary, dead-heading is carried out meticulously throughout the summer.

The layout of the garden almost disappears completely under luxuriant vegetation during the summer. The area to the south of the house, with its paved enclosures, quadrant of Irish yews and pergola was designed by Countess Sophie Benckendorff (1855–1928), after removing farm buildings from the site. The Countess was the last Tsarist Ambassadress to the Court of St James.

Soon after Humphrey Brooke inherited the garden his increasing collection of rare old roses led him to expand it, planting in the former vegetable garden, along the lawn and in the sunken garden on the north side of the house. He was one of the few rose enthusiasts to remain uninfluenced by changing fashions, continuing to grow Hybrid Perpetual roses, Chinas and some of the earliest Hybrid Teas simply because he enjoyed them. He has also been instrumental in rescuing and reinstating the rambler 'White Flight', 'Hunslett Moss', one of the earliest of English Moss roses, and 'Surpassing Beauty' which he discovered growing on the church at Woolverstone in Suffolk.

Lime Kiln does indeed house a distinguished collection of roses, but it is very much more than a collection. Other plants include *Buddleia alternifolia* growing as a small tree, lilacs, philadelphus, *Hydrangea sargentiana*, escallonias, and tree peonies, and the whole is surrounded by mature trees, some of which have reached a stage where they cast too much shade for the roses. Yet the roses literally rise to the occasion, clambering to the sunlight above and through the trees and shrubs. The idea of luxuriant planting within a formal framework is carried to its furthest limits and the result is magical.

Sadly, Humphrey Brooke died in December 1988. Let us hope that his roses will always remain at Lime Kiln as his memorial.

SUDELEY CASTLE, WINCHCOMBE, GLOUCESTERSHIRE

Comfortably settled in a broad valley and sheltered by wooded Cotswold hills, Sudeley is one of those rare houses where history is almost tangible. The warmth of its golden stone seems to radiate memories of every phase of the castle's development: the lost medieval village; the tenth- or eleventh-century Manor House; the great building phase in the fifteenth century under Ralph le Boteler when the castle, the adjacent church of St Mary and the handsome tithe barn were all constructed; the darker days of the Civil War when the church was desecrated and much of the castle destroyed. It is thanks to the vision of the Dent family who bought the castle in the 1830s, that the remains of the old castle and tithe barn were preserved and restoration carried out to bring the property back into use as a family home, which it remains today.

Not only the architectural styles of different centuries, but the personalities of different owners of Sudeley are reflected in its buildings and in its gardens. Among them was Catherine Parr, Henry VIII's last queen. Distinguished for her learning and her piety, Catherine lived at Sudeley with Thomas Seymour whom she married after Henry's death. She gave a home there to the sadly fated Lady Jane Grey.

The gardens were laid out towards the end of the last century by another distinguished owner and patroness of Sudeley, Emma Dent, as part of the continuing restoration work on the castle. They include the Queen's Garden, named in honour of Catherine Parr, and set out as a formal parterre, its design based on fragments of an earlier Tudor garden discovered on the same site. Today, Lady Ashcombe, the present owner of the Castle has chosen the Queen's Garden as the ideal site for a rose garden, planned and planted in 1988. In re-planting this garden, creating a new private garden and adding to the planting elsewhere in the grounds, Lady Ashcombe is following the tradition of innovation and improvement followed by previous owners, which has produced the richness and variety which bring so many visitors to Sudeley.

The parterre of the Queen's Garden is enclosed to the north

OVERLEAF

The author's planting plan for the Queen's Garden at Sudeley Castle.

155

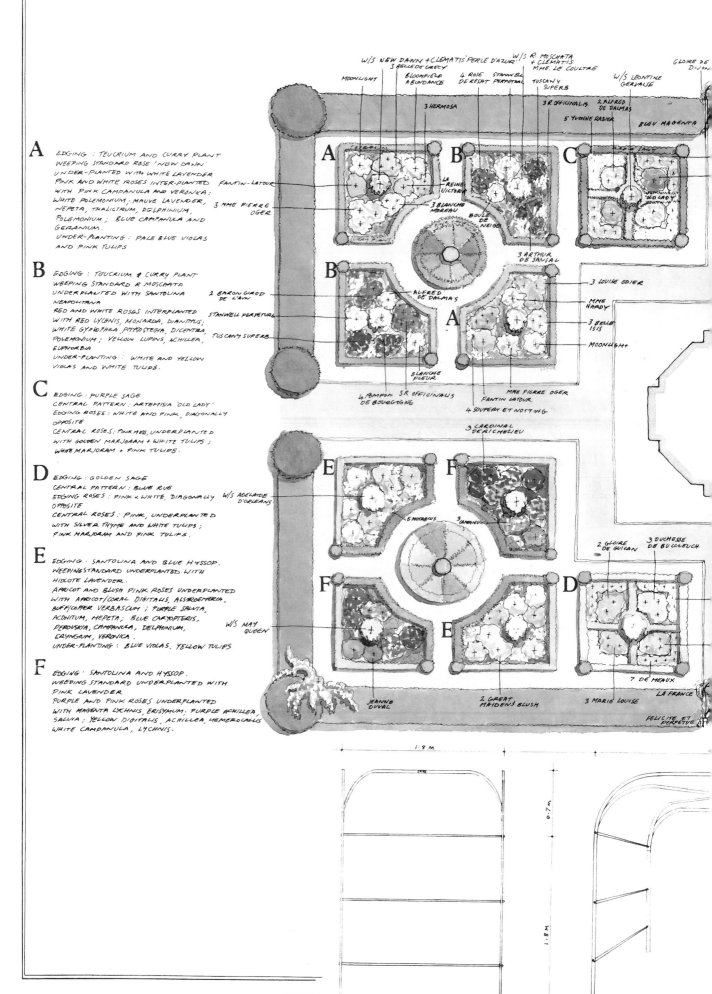

A
EDGING : TEUCRIUM AND CURRY PLANT
WEEPING STANDARD ROSE 'NEW DAWN'
UNDER-PLANTED WITH WHITE LAVENDER
PINK AND WHITE ROSES INTER-PLANTED
WITH PINK CAMPANULA AND VERONICA;
WHITE POLEMONIUM; MAUVE LAVENDER,
NEPETA, THALICTRUM, DELPHINIUM,
POLEMONIUM; BLUE CAMPANULA AND
GERANIUM.
UNDER-PLANTING: PALE BLUE VIOLAS
AND PINK TULIPS

B
EDGING : TEUCRIUM & CURRY PLANT
WEEPING STANDARD R.MOSCHATA
UNDERPLANTED WITH SANTOLINA
NEAPOLITANA
RED AND WHITE ROSES INTERPLANTED
WITH RED LYCHNIS, MONARDA, DIANTHUS;
WHITE GYPSOPHILA, PHYSOSTEGIA, DICENTRA,
POLEMONIUM; YELLOW LUPINS, ACHILLEA,
EUPHORBIA
UNDER-PLANTING: WHITE AND YELLOW
VIOLAS AND WHITE TULIPS.

C
EDGING : PURPLE SAGE
CENTRAL PATTERN : ARTEMISIA 'OLD LADY'
EDGING ROSES : WHITE AND PINK, DIAGONALLY
OPPOSITE
CENTRAL ROSES: PINK MOSS, UNDERPLANTED
WITH GOLDEN MARJORAM + WHITE TULIPS;
WHITE MARJORAM + PINK TULIPS.

D
EDGING : GOLDEN SAGE
CENTRAL PATTERN : BLUE RUE
EDGING ROSES : PINK & WHITE, DIAGONALLY
OPPOSITE
CENTRAL ROSES : PINK, UNDERPLANTED
WITH SILVER THYME AND WHITE TULIPS;
PINK MARJORAM AND PINK TULIPS.

E
EDGING : SANTOLINA AND BLUE HYSSOP.
WEEPING STANDARD UNDERPLANTED WITH
HIDCOTE LAVENDER.
APRICOT AND BLUSH PINK ROSES UNDERPLANTED
WITH APRICOT/CORAL DIGITALIS, ALSTROEMERIA,
BUFF/COPPER VERBASCUM; PURPLE SALVIA,
ACONITUM, NEPETA; BLUE CARYOPTERIS,
PEROVSKIA, CAMPANULA, DELPHINIUM,
ERYNGIUM, VERONICA.
UNDER-PLANTING : BLUE VIOLAS, YELLOW TULIPS.

F
EDGING : SANTOLINA AND HYSSOP.
WEEDING STANDARD UNDERPLANTED WITH
PINK LAVENDER
PURPLE AND PINK ROSES UNDERPLANTED
WITH MAGENTA LYCHNIS, ERISYMUM; PURPLE ACHILLEA,
SALVIA; YELLOW DIGITALIS, ACHILLEA, HEMEROCALLIS
WHITE CAMPANULA, LYCHNIS.

SCALE 1 : 20   SIDE ELEVATION   ROSE ARCHE S : FA

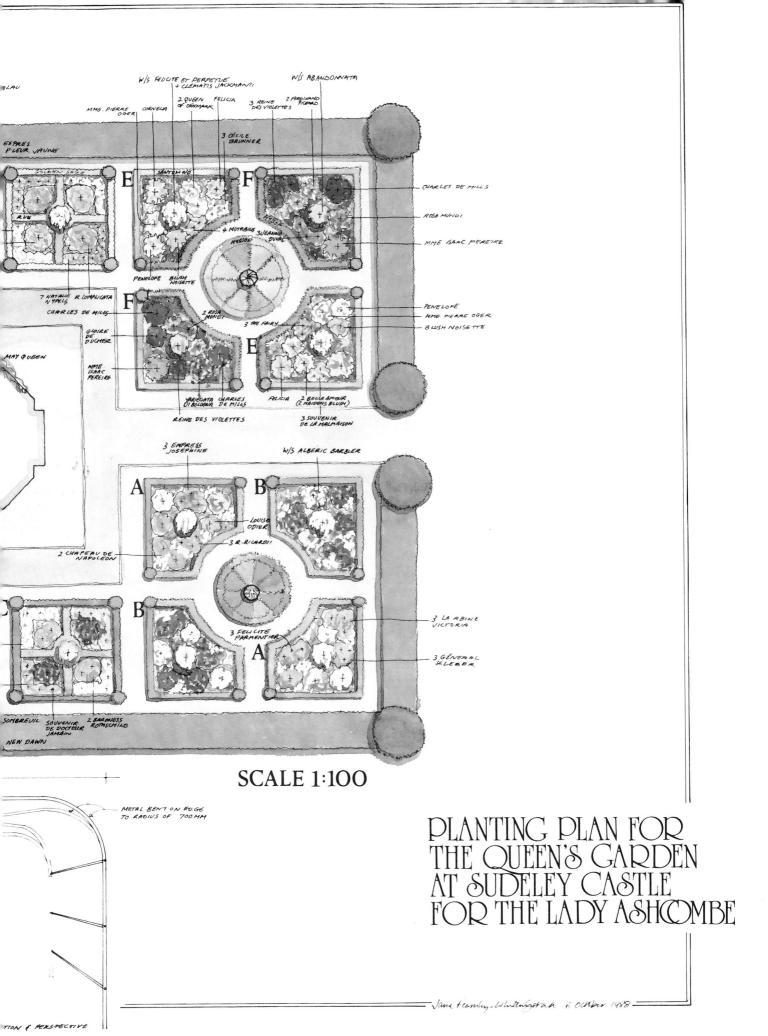

BLAU

ESPRES
FLEUR JAUNE

GOLDEN SAGE

RUE

MMG. PIERRE
OGER

CORNELA

w/s FEUCITE ET PERPETUE
+ CLEMATIS JACKMANII

SANTOLINO

2 QUEEN
OF DENMARK

FELICIA

3 CÉCILE
BRUNNER

w/s ABANDONNATA

3 REINE
DES VIOLETTES

2 FERDINAND
PICHARD

CHARLES DE MILLS

ROSA MUNDI

MME ISAAC PEREIRE

E   F

4 MUTABILIS   3 JEANNE
HYBRID   DUVAL

PENELOPE   BLUSH
NOISETTE

7 NATALIE   R. COMPLICATA
NYPELS

CHARLES DE MILLS

GLOIRE
DE DUCHER

MAY QUEEN

MME
ISAAC
PEREIRE

F

2 ROSA
MUNDI

3 THE FAIRY

E

PENELOPE
MME PIERRE OGER
BLUSH NOISETTE

VARIEGATA   CHARLES
DI BOLOGNA   DE MILS

REINE DES VIOLETTES

FELICIA

2 BELLE AMOUR
(2 MAIDENS BLUSH)

3 SOUVENIR
DE LA MALMAISON

3 EMPRESS
JOSEPHINE

w/s ALBERIC BARBIER

A   B

LOUISE
ODIER

3 R. RICARDII

2 CHAPEAU DE
NAPOLEON

C

B   A

3 FELICITE
PARMENTIER

3 LA REINE
VICTORIA

3 GENERAL
KLEBER

SOMBREUIL

SOUVENIR
DE DOCTEUR
JAMAIN

2 BARONESS
ROTHSCHILD

NEW DAWN

SCALE 1:100

METAL BENT ON EDGE
TO RADIUS OF 700 MM

PLANTING PLAN FOR
THE QUEEN'S GARDEN
AT SUDELEY CASTLE
FOR THE LADY ASHCOMBE

Jane Fearnley-Whittingstall   6 October 1988

SECTION & PERSPECTIVE

and south by great double yew hedges with secret tunnelled walks through their centres. From the west it can be seen through the splendid gothic windows which are part of the ruined banqueting hall of Ralph Boteler's castle of the 1440s. There are raised grass walks on the east and south sides, where the view from above makes the pattern of the beds clear. In the new rose garden, the original pattern remains intact. The central, focal point of the garden is an octagonal pool surrounded by graceful stone balustrading and set in a plain, square lawn. The surrounding beds are laid out in the classic pattern of a circle within a square, divided by gravelled walks and subdivided by grass paths. These beds were originally planted with blocks of sweet smelling herbs: rosemary, purple and pink lavender, purple and golden sage, hyssop, germander, rue, *Artemisia* 'Old Man' and 'Old Lady'. The herbs have been retained in the central circular pattern of each quartered section, where they surround stone urns, planted with seasonal flowers. The scent of the herbs mingles with that of the roses. Their dense, tidy form gives structure and solidity and, with their long history as garden plants, they anchor the Queen's Garden to its Tudor origins.

Sudeley's emblem is a Tudor rose, but the roses in the Queen's Garden reflect every period of the Castle's development, from Tudor times to the present. The planting is planned not according to rose history but by colour, making a diagonal pattern within each square, with blocks of purple-shaded roses, of pinks and whites, and of yellows and apricots. Beneath the roses are early-flowering tulips and violas to extend the season of colour, and among them are herbaceous plants, emphasising the colour scheme of the roses or contrasting with it, in accordance with some of the ideas about colour outlined in Chapter 12.

There are many roses elsewhere at Sudeley, including a collection of wild roses from many parts of the world in the tithe barn ruin, climbers on the walls of the banqueting hall and others in mixed borders and in the white border of the church. As the rose garden matures, it will bring all these strands together into a celebration of roses from medieval times to the present, emulating in colour and scent the rich variety of the history of the castle and its owners through the centuries.

ANDOVER HOUSE, NEAR MALMESBURY, WILTSHIRE

One of the advantages of roses is the speed with which they bestow maturity on a garden. It would be impossible to guess that the Countess of Suffolk and Berkshire began making the garden at Andover House in the early 1980s, for it is already well established enough to be an inspiring source of ideas for colour schemes and companion plants for roses.

An arch leads to the stables through a high wall planted with the lovely buff-apricot single-flowered climber 'Meg', and the amazingly floriferous 'Coral Dawn'. The arch is framed with beds of 'Golden Showers' and 'Iceberg' edged with catmint, and yellow 'Arthur Bell' and 'Korresia' with blue geraniums. 'Meg' appears again in the entrance courtyard, joined by the more coppery 'Schoolgirl'. Pink 'Constance Spry' with her heavy, sumptuous blooms frames a gothic window, and the richness of these colours on the walls is tempered by the soft, pinkish grey-green of *Vitis henryana*. The beds in this courtyard are densely planted with yellow and pink roses: 'Canary Bird', golden 'Graham Thomas', light salmon-pink 'Fritz Nobis', and 'Constance Spry' grown as a shrub. The yellows are reinforced by shrubs: a golden berberis, *Potentilla* 'Primrose Beauty', and *Philadelphus coronarius* 'Aureus'. The bold foliage of *Bergenia* 'Silberlicht', *Euphorbia characias wulfenii*, *Alchemilla mollis*, *Hosta fortunei* 'Albopicta' and blue rue provides contrast. *Lilium regale* adds its scent and stately flower spikes and campanulas contribute touches of strong purple.

In the next courtyard purple-reds, rich pinks, violets and blues dominate: roses 'Charles de Mills' and 'Aloha' are planted with *Ceanothus* 'Cascade'; 'Madame Isaac Pereire', 'Common Moss', 'Tuscany Superb' and striped 'Rosa Mundi' and 'Ferdinand Pichard' are lightened by 'Moonlight' and 'Penelope'.

There are three rose gardens at Andover House, all circular in shape and all differently planted. The first is set against a background of philadelphus and *Cornus alba* 'Elegantissima' with mature trees beyond. The second, tiny rose garden is approached through a newly constructed and planted pergola. It is a simple

159

circle of 'Ballerina' with catmint and helianthemum 'Wisley Prim-rose'.

These two little gardens are echoes of the main rose garden. Encircled by pleached limes underplanted with a hedge of *Lavandula spica*, the two inner circles are box edged, and planted with massed 'Nathalie Nypels' and 'Pearl Drift' punctuated by standards of 'Ballerina'. The outer ring is filled with scented old roses, among them 'Souvenir du Docteur Jamain', 'Paul Neyron', 'Fantin-Latour', 'Madame Legras' and 'Louise Odier'. Planted among the roses are nepeta, alchemilla, pinks, *Artemisia schmidtiana*, *Linum perenne*, *Geranium renardii*, *Lilium regale*, *Salvia × superba* 'Lubeca', *Veronica austriaca* 'Royal Blue', *Veronica gentianoides* and many violas.

Other imaginative ideas with roses at Andover House include a stone trough filled with 'Pink Bells'; a standard 'Nozomi' underplanted with prostrate 'Nozomi'; the shrub rose 'Fountain' with its huge, crimson, continuous flowers, trained as a climber; neat semi-circles of pink, white, or blue lavender planted at the feet of climbing roses; and a long wall of white climbers, climbing 'Iceberg', 'Paul's Lemon Pillar' and 'Albéric Barbier' alternating with the golden hop.

The achievement here, in such a short time, will inspire anyone who is setting out to garden with roses for the first time.

The circular rose garden.

HELMINGHAM HALL, HELMINGHAM, SUFFOLK

There are two rose gardens at Helmingham, both formal, both appropriate to the lovely moated house, built of pinky-red brick between 1480 and 1510, and each very different in character.

The garden to the east of the house was laid out comparatively recently, in 1982, on a site where there has always been a garden from the time the house was built. It lies below a grass walk, so that the pattern of beds can be clearly seen from above and, at a greater distance, from the windows of the house, across the moat. Lady Tollemache's intention was to create something that was close to the kind of garden a Tudor Tollemache might have made, but one that would include old, scented shrub roses. She sought help from Lady Salisbury in devising an historically authentic plan and in choosing plants that would be suitable for the period. Drawings of the scheme were made by H. Dalton Clifford and the plan was transferred from paper to the level site between the moat and the coach-house pond. Six years later, it looks as if it must have been there always.

At the west end, immediately below the walk, so that the symmetrical design can be appreciated, are two knot patterns made in clipped box. Each pattern is divided into four squares; that on the south side is planted with herbs. Two of the four squares on the north side show the pattern of the Tollemache fret which can also be seen in the brickwork of the house. The other two patterns are based on Lord and Lady Tollemache's initials, a 'T' and an 'A'. The interstices contain plants that were introduced to England before 1750. The knot beds and all the rose beds have a neat brick edging, the kind of finishing detail that is not always noticeable but which makes a great difference to the general effect.

Beyond the knots are two simple rectangular beds edged with catmint and each planted with fifteen plants of 'Rosa Mundi'. The eastern half of the garden is laid out in a pattern combining the square, the circle and the cross, the three archetypal decorative themes. The four outer beds are edged in lavender and planted with roses, one of Alba and Scottish roses, one of Centifolia and Moss roses, one of Gallicas, Damasks and Bourbons, one of China and Hybrid Perpetual roses. Among the roses are planted white foxgloves, blue and white *Campanula persicifolia*, *Alchemilla mollis*, purple violas and several species of geranium. This dense planting in a restricted colour range is very effective. To support roses with a lax habit of growth, and train roses as an alternative to pegging down so that they flower all the way along their stems, Lady Tollemache has devised a metal support which works very well. It consists of a strong central rod with wires radiating out from it. The pliable young shoots of the roses are bent over and tied in to the wires.

The inner beds are edged in hyssop and planted with a romantic profusion of small shrubs and herbaceous plants spanning the seasons, from early hellebores to late fuchsias and hibiscus. In the centre, and the focal point for the whole garden, is a brick pattern of a circle within a square within a circle, closely planted with golden thyme through which narcissi, tulips and lilies grow at different seasons. From the central circle a stone figure of Flora holding a garland of roses tranquilly surveys the scene.

The garden is enclosed by yew hedges, and paths lead from it to the old stables where climbing roses cover the walls, to the swimming pool enclosure where species roses grow in grass, and to the coach-house pond where a huge rose 'Cerise Bouquet' is reflected from the bank.

The second rose garden at Helmingham is on the opposite, west side of the house. It was made by Dinah, Lady Tollemache (the mother of the present Lord Tollemache) in 1965 to replace labour-intensive herbaceous borders. The roses are all Hybrid Musks, the familiar 'Penelope', 'Cornelia' and 'Felicia' and other less well-known members of the group: 'Danäe', 'Thisbe', 'Daybreak', 'Kathleen' and 'Nur Mahal'. The garden is a wide rectangle, more open and on a larger scale than the parterre on the east side of the house. It is approached from the north or the south by a wide grass walk with majestic classical stone figures at each end, and across a wide grass 'bridge' spanning a secondary moat with water lilies lying on the still water and grassy banks dotted with primroses and narcissi. A central vista across the wide lawn leads through fine wrought iron gates to a large walled garden. A box-edged parterre with a central stone urn is laid out at each side of the lawn. The parterre beds used to be filled with annual bedding plants, but now there is a simple, permanent planting of

Plan showing the Tudor Knot and Rose Garden at Helmingham Hall.

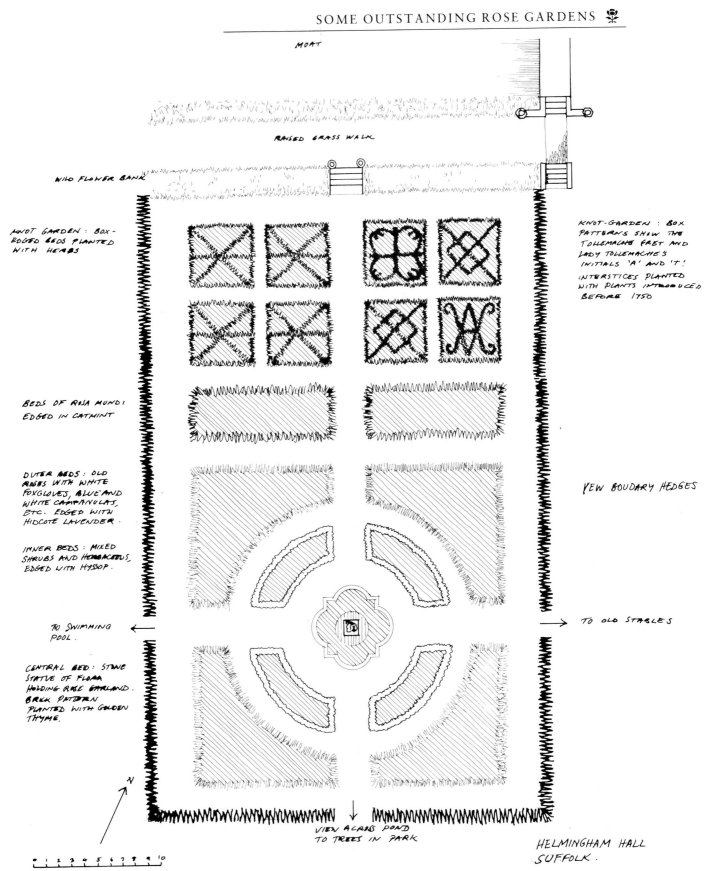

MOAT

RAISED GRASS WALK

WILD FLOWER BANK

KNOT GARDEN: BOX-
EDGED BEDS PLANTED
WITH HERBS

KNOT-GARDEN: BOX
PATTERNS SHOW THE
TOLLEMACHE FRET AND
LADY TOLLEMACHE'S
INITIALS 'A' AND 'T'.
INTERSTICES PLANTED
WITH PLANTS INTRODUCED
BEFORE 1750

BEDS OF ROSA MUNDI
EDGED IN CATMINT

OUTER BEDS: OLD
ROSES WITH WHITE
FOXGLOVES, BLUE AND
WHITE CAMPANULAS,
ETC. EDGED WITH
HIDCOTE LAVENDER.

YEW BOUDARY HEDGES

INNER BEDS: MIXED
SHRUBS AND HERBACEOUS,
EDGED WITH HYSSOP.

TO SWIMMING
POOL.

TO OLD STABLES

CENTRAL BED: STONE
STATUE OF FLORA
HOLDING ROSE GARLAND.
BRICK PATTERN
PLANTED WITH GOLDEN
THYME.

N

VIEW ACROSS POND
TO TREES IN PARK

HELMINGHAM HALL
SUFFOLK.

0 1 2 3 4 5 6 7 8 9 10
METRES

blue violas, which is, perhaps, an improvement.

The Hybrid Musk roses grow in wide borders beneath the brick walls on either side of the gates and at each end of the lawn. These beds are completely carpeted with London pride, which makes a dense, weed-smothering ground cover but does not prevent peonies, *Campanula lactiflora* and Japanese anemones from growing through. The roses are a magnificent sight over a long period, spanning the season of both the campanulas and the anemones.

Beyond the wrought iron gates the walled garden, the wall of which dates from 1742, has been used to grow vegetables since Elizabethan times and still is today. The central path is bordered by herbaceous plants backed with climbing roses trained on wires and here, and on the south side of the wall, are several rare and interesting varieties, including 'Kitchener of Khartoum', 'Richmond', 'Morlettii', 'John Hopper' and *R. multiflora* 'Cathayensis'.

A hedge of 'Rosa Mundi' divides the herb knots from the Rose Garden with its stone figure of Flora. White foxgloves are planted among the roses.

GOODNESTONE PARK, NEAR CANTERBURY, KENT

Five miles from Canterbury and about the same distance from the M2 motorway, Goodnestone (pronounced Gunston) Park feels a hundred miles from everywhere and more than a hundred years away from the 1980s, such is the timeless tranquillity of its gardens and parkland. Like so many places in the south and east of England, it suffered sad losses of beautiful and mature trees in the Great Storm of October 1987, but many remain to give the fine eighteenth-century house and its surroundings a mature and handsome setting.

The house is sited above a sweep of lawn to look out across a hidden, sunken lane to the southern part of the park. Today the lawn is softened and the house framed by great clumps of 'Nevada' and 'Maigold' roses, and the steps up to the house are framed by groups of 'Tour de Malakoff', 'Trier', 'Pax', 'Blanchefleur' and 'Fantin-Latour'.

The vista to the church continues through the three walled gardens.

The Bridges family, whose daughter married Jane Austen's brother, built the house at a time when it was fashionable to surround great houses with landscape and to site the vegetable, fruit and flower gardens where they would not interrupt the view. So it is only after some exploration of the informal groups of shrubs and trees and the small woodland garden, that you come upon the opening in the mellow brick wall which leads into a private world of roses. At first you think you have arrived in a spacious, but not forbiddingly large walled garden with a pretty vista along its west to east axis focusing on the church tower at some distance. But as you reach the opening at the far end of the walled garden, you find that the church is not much nearer, and that you are entering a second walled garden; and that, in turn, gives on to a third.

Each enclosure is treated differently, but all three are full of roses. Their design and planting are the work of Lady FitzWalter whose husband inherited the house in 1955, together with a derelict garden completely overgrown with brambles and nettles. The slow and painstaking work of restoration has resulted in a garden of beauty and distinction in many different ways, but perhaps this series of walled gardens is the loveliest part of all.

The first enclosure is entered through an arch in the brick wall, in the north west corner, and a straight walk runs the length of the north (south facing) wall, with similar arches piercing the walls into the second and third garden. Part of the charm of the gardens lies in the attention to detail in the built elements, as in these arches. This arched walk is secondary to the main axis of the garden, which is a broad, grassed walk between two straight borders, that on the north side being backed by a yew hedge which separates it from the secondary path and forms a background to the old roses. At intervals, tripods draped with clematis rise above the old roses, which include the crimson and purples of 'M. Pélisson', 'Tuscany', 'Charles de Mills', the Moss rose 'Nuits de Young', and 'Cardinal de Richelieu', mingling with pink, striped and white roses. Modern roses looking at home in such company include 'Alchemist' and 'Aloha'. The roses are set off by foreground planting of hostas, astrantias, aquilegias, thalictrum, many varieties of geranium and the grey foliage of lavender, rue, artemisias and *Stachys lanata*.

The second walled garden is more elaborate, with a formal

THIRD WALLED GARDEN: VEGETABLE PLOTS FLANKED BY FLOWERING SHRUBS AND SHRUB ROSES. WALK TO ARBOUR BORDERED WITH FLORIBUNDA ROSES ENCLOSED BY LAVENDER HEDGES

SECOND WALLED GARDEN: SHRUB ROSES, BOX-EDGED HERBACEOUS BEDS, ROSE ARCHES; A WEEPING SILVER PEAR TREES. ROSES ON WALLS

FIRST WALLED GARDEN: SHRUB ROSE WALK BACKED BY YEW HEDGE

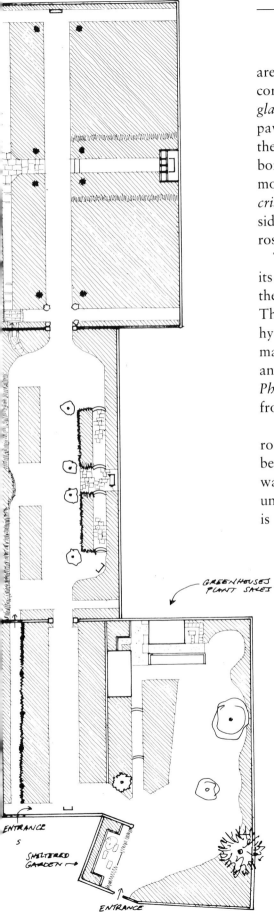

area of box-edged beds with weeping silver pear trees at their corners, backed by a paved walk under arches supporting *Rosa glauca* (a pretty and unusual way to use it). There is a central paved area with 'Ballerina' behind it and 'Emily Gray' climbing the wall. Against the wall opposite, the narrow, lavender-edged border widens to accommodate a group of 'Celestial' and 'Hermosa' with lavender, an edging of blue grass, and *Solanum crispum* 'Glasnevin' on the wall behind. Two large beds on each side of this group are planted with lilacs, philadelphus, Rugosa roses, lilies and phlox.

The last of the three gardens is really the vegetable garden, but its south facing wall is planted with roses and the end wall, with the church rising in the background, with an immense wisteria. The central walk is lined with shrub roses, peonies, cistuses, hydrangeas and *Weigela florida* 'Variegata'. In the centre of the main vegetable plot is a little rose garden, hedged with lavender and planted with 'Chanelle' and 'Willhire County' Floribundas, *Philadelphus* 'Belle Etoile' and *P.* 'Manteau d'Hermine', and, in front, *Geranium renardii* and dark red herbaceous potentillas.

The success of these gardens is partly due to the fact that the roses and other shrubs are planted in bold groups so that the beds and borders never look fussy or spotty, and due also to the way that the long vista to the church is allowed to continue uninterrupted for the entire length of the three walled gardens. It is a much-photographed view, and rightly so.

Plan showing the layout of the walled gardens.

167

CHILCOMBE HOUSE, CHILCOMBE, DORSET

Caryl and John Hubbard came to this remote and lovely place in 1970. Their house, the adjoining church and some farm buildings, built of the local, weathered, grey stone, are all that now remain of the lost village of Chilcombe. It is hard to imagine the village street in which the house once stood, high in the Dorset downland between Bridport and Dorchester.

There are spectacular views to the surrounding hills and the sea. The garden, by contrast, is enclosed and intimate. It invites close-up inspection. The details which will please the observant visitor include exciting and unexpected juxtapositions of colours, leaf shapes or plant forms; the variety of building materials (stone, brick, cobbles), set out in varied patterns on paths and beneath arbours; a bank of thyme; a lichen-encrusted stone seat, and, of course, details displayed by the old roses which dominate the garden in June: the hair-line white edging to the red petals of 'Baron Girod de l'Ain', or the shifting shades of lavender, grey, purple and dusty pink in the fading flowers of 'Camaieux'. Such delightful vignettes are welded into unity by the layout. The main part of the garden is quartered and re-quartered in the Paradise Garden tradition, each rectangle distinguished from the rest by means of its enclosure and by the design and planting within.

The garden is entered either from the house by a short flight of stone steps or from the paved courtyard outside the front door. Both entrances lead on to a wide, walled lawn framing the east front of the house. Just inside the door from the courtyard is a favourite sitting place with a table and chairs set on stone paving in the sheltered angle of the wall where the trickle and splash of water from a wall-mounted dolphin fountain soothes the ear and roses glimpsed over the wall give scent as well as colour. A long, low wall running parallel to the house separates the lawn from the garden beyond. Immediately below the wall the soft pink rose 'Fantin-Latour' alternates with blue-purple *Solanum crispum* 'Glasnevin'.

Two openings in the wall lead down short flights of steps to the garden below which slopes gently away. At right angles to the wall, the main axis of the garden, running from west to east, is

One of the many rose-framed vistas through pergola and arches. In the foreground, strong shapes of pale yellow *Sisyrinchium striatum*. On the pergola, 'Mme Alice Garnier', 'Frances E. Lester' and 'Goldfinch'.

punctuated by pairs of Irish yews planted by the Hubbards. A secondary and parallel axis, in line with the door to the house, is marked by two massive mature Irish yews of an earlier date. This walk is shaded by a simple pergola constructed from wooden poles and covered in honeysuckle, jasmine, clematis and, of course, roses: 'Bleu Magenta', 'Madame Alice Garnier', 'Frances E. Lester', 'The Garland' and 'Félicité et Perpétue'.

If you take the grass path along the main axis and turn left under an arch of 'Goldfinch' and 'Tour de Malakoff', you will find yourself in the first quarter of the garden, enclosed by espaliered pear trees with rose 'Reine des Violettes' trained through them, and under-planted with anaphalis and veronica on one side and nepeta on the other. I would happily travel to Dorset just to see this combination. The quarter is halved by a walk edged with lavender, purple sage and irises; the centre of one half is marked by a standard white wisteria underplanted with geum, the other by a stone sundial surrounded with polygonum.

This green enclosure is divided by a grass walk with tall double hedges from the vegetable garden. Here, neat plots are subdivided by brick and turf paths, and the tidy rows of vegetables can be admired from the scented shade of an arbour in the angle of the two boundary walls where a monolithic table is roofed over with honeysuckle and the rose 'Bobbie James'.

A broad grass walk leads between an 'Albertine'-covered wall and a row of raspberry canes to another resting place. A seat backed by the fragrant, nearly thornless violet-purple rambler 'Veilchenblau' commands the main vista back towards the house, framed by pairs of Irish yews. The orchard is to the left, with rambling roses tumbling out of fruit trees and Species roses arching over the meadow grasses to display their hips in autumn. To the right is a broad bed of shrub roses including 'Petite de Hollande', its prim little rosettes contrasting with the lush blooms of 'Mrs John Laing'.

Beyond the orchard, the quartet of gardens-within-a-garden is completed by a formal area of eight small beds planted with small shrubs and herbaceous perennials and divided by a double cross of patterned cobble paths. This little garden is contained on one side by a pergola of roses, honeysuckle and jasmine, and on the other by espaliered fruit trees entwined with clematis. The path under the pergola leads back to the wide lawn immediately below the house.

On the south west side of the house there is a sheltered court-yard protected by the house and conservatory. Here box-edged beds hold smaller-growing roses: 'The Fairy', 'Yvonne Rabier', the strangely coloured 'Président de Sèze' and a pretty little unidentified white rambler.

One of the delights of this garden is that there are plenty of strategically placed seats. They provide focal points for vistas and a solid contrast to the shifting textures of foliage. Moreover, whatever direction the wind blows from, there is always a sheltered place where you can sit in sun or shade and enjoy the interlocking patterns of scent, colour and form.

A Selection of Roses

In cold climates roses are at risk not so much from the hard winter frosts, which occur whilst the plants are dormant, as from harsh winds and the alternate freezing and thawing when late frosts strike in the spring and early summer months. Alba roses and Gallicas tolerate high altitudes and windswept sites; most climbing roses will come through hard winters and the Rugosas are particularly hardy. But all benefit if wind protection can be provided by a belt of evergreen trees and shrubs, and in areas where the temperature drops below 10° Fahrenheit (−12° Centigrade) smaller bushes should be covered with earth mounds and taller plants wrapped in layers of straw, dry bracken or sacking held in place with an outer wrapping of polythene or plastic. Treated in this way in Sweden, Hybrid Tea and Floribunda roses survive temperatures of −30° Centigrade.

In tropical climates, fragile young rose plants need shading from the hot sun. Many roses, particularly those of yellow and orange shades, fail to colour fully in the heat, but tropical conditions provide an opportunity to enjoy the tender roses which in colder areas need to be grown under glass, such as Tea roses and some of the Noisette and China roses.

Roses prefer a slightly acid loam with a fairly high clay content. Most will perform well in less than ideal conditions, but where the soil is very poor and sandy R. *pimpinellifolia* (also known as Scotch or Burnet) roses do well, as do Albas, Rugosas, Gallicas and R. *virginiana*. In water-logged soil the two American species R. *nitida* and R. *palustris* (the Swamp rose) should succeed.

The one situation that roses cannot tolerate is dense shade, but many roses are happy in a position that only gets sun for part of the day, or in the dappled shade of woodland with a light canopy. There are also several climbing roses which are happy growing on a north-facing wall. Those roses which are tolerant of some shade are marked with an * in the list below.

Where there is more than one limiting factor, for example poor soil and shade on the same site, the Albas and Rugosas are a good bet. These two sturdy classes of rose are also disease resistant and worth trying in the most hostile situations.

Key to tables following

Bourb Bourbon, **Cent** Centifolia, **Cl** Climber, **Dam** Damask, **Gall** Gallica, **Fl** Floribunda, **HM** Hybrid Musk, **HP** Hybrid Perpetual, **Port** Portland, **R** Rambler, **Rug** Rugosa, **Sh** Shrub, **Sp** Species

* denotes a rose which tolerates some shade

15 ft/4.5 m or more: suitable for training into trees, on arbours or on large walls.

Adélaide d'Orléans	Cl, weeping standard	15 × 10 ft (4.5 × 3 m)	Semi-double, small, pinkish-white, in clusters. Evergreen.
Albéric Barbier	R, weeping standard	15 × 10 ft (4.5 × 3 m)	Semi-double, small, yellow-white, in clusters. No scent. Repeat-flowering. Attractive foliage.
Félicité et Perpétue	R, weeping standard, *	15 × 10 ft (4.5 × 3 m)	Double, small, cream-white in clusters. Attractive foliage.
Kiftsgate	Sp, *	30 × 20 ft (9 × 7 m)	Single, creamy in huge clusters. Attractive foliage and hips. Good autumn colour.
Long John Silver	Cl, *	18 × 10 ft (5.4 × 3 m)	Double, large, white.
Paul's Lemon Pillar	Cl, *	15 × 10 ft (4.5 × 3 m)	Double, very large HT, lemon-white

Height 8 to 15 ft/2.5 to 4.5 m, suitable for arches, pergolas and walls or pillars, or as shrubs if so described.

Aimée Vibert	Cl, weeping standard, *	12 × 10 ft (3.6 × 3 m)	Double, in small clusters. Repeat-flowering.
Mme Alfred Carrière	Cl, *	12 × 10 ft (3.6 × 3 m)	Double, pinkish-white, in clusters. Fairly continuous flowering.
Mrs Herbert Stevens	Cl, *	12 × 8 ft (3.6 × 2.5 m)	Double, shapely HT, plentiful. Repeat-flowering.
Sombreuil	Cl, needs warm, sheltered site, *	8 × 5 ft (2.5 × 1.5 m)	Double, repeat-flowering

Shrubs 4 to 8 ft/1.2 to 2.5 m tall

Alba Semi-Plena	Alba, pre C16th, *	8 × 5 ft (2.5 × 1.5 m)	Semi-double. Attractive foliage and hips.
Blanc Double de Coubert	Rug, good in pots, much loved rose, *	5 × 4 ft (1.5 × 1.2 m)	Semi-double. Attractive hips. Repeat-flowering.
Frau Karl Druschki	HP	5 × 3 ft (1.5 × 1 m)	Double, no scent. Repeat-flowering.
Heather Muir	Sh, hybrid of *R. sericea*, *	8 × 6 ft (2.5 × 1.8 m)	Single, early flowering, unscented. Attractive foliage and hips.
Hebe's Lip	Sh, *	4 × 4 ft (1.2 × 1.2 m)	Single, with red-edged petals. No scent.
Iceberg	Fl, standard good in pots	5 × 3 ft (1.5 × 1 m)	Double, most free flowering white rose.
Mme Hardy	Dam, *	5 × 5 ft (1.5 × 1.5 m)	Double, green eye to flowers.

Nevada	**Sh**	8 × 7 ft (2.5 × 2 m)	Single, large cream flowers. Fairly continuous flowering.
Prosperity	**HM,** arching habit, *	5 × 4 ft (1.5 × 1.2 m)	Double. Repeat-flowering.
R. fedtschenkoana	**Sp,** *	5 × 4 ft (1.5 × 1.2 m)	Single. Repeat-flowering. No scent. Attractive grey foliage. Hips.
R. rugosa alba	**Sp,** *	7 × 6 ft (2 × 1.8 m)	Single. Repeat-flowering. No scent. Big red hips overlap with late flowers.
R. wichuriana	**Sp,** prostrate but will climb, *	6 × 20 ft (1.8 × 7 m)	Single.
Stanwell Perpetual	**Sh,** standard, *	5 × 4 ft (1.5 × 1.2 m)	Double, blush white. Fairly continuous flowering.
White Spray	**Sh,** good in pots	4 × 4 ft (1.2 × 1.2 m)	Double. No scent. Fairly continuous flowering.
White Wings	**HT,** plant in groups	4 × 3 ft (1.2 × 0.9 m)	Single. Repeat-flowering.

Height 1 ft/0.3 m to 4 ft/1.2 m Plant in groups of 3 or more, except for spreading varieties.

Lady Romsey	**Fl,** good in pots	2 × 2 ft (0.6 × 0.6 m)	Double, apricot-white. Fairly continuous flowering.
Little White Pet	**Sh,** standard, ground cover *	2 × 2 ft (0.6 × 0.6 m)	Double, prolific, small pompoms. Fairly continuous flowering.
Margaret Merrill	**Fl,** good in pots	4 × 3 ft (1.2 × 0.9 m)	Double, pinkish-white, shapely. Fairly continuous flowering.
Partridge	**Sh,** ground cover, *	2 × 10 ft (0.6 × 3.0 m)	Single, small flowers in clusters, no scent, procumbent. Repeat-flowering. Attractive foliage.
Snow Carpet	**Sh,** standard, ground cover, good in pots,*	1 × 3 ft (0.3 × 0.9 m)	Double, no scent, procumbent. Repeat-flowering. Attractive foliage.
Swany	**Sh,** weeping standard, ground cover, good in pots, *	3 × 5 ft (0.9 × 1.5 m)	Double, no scent, procumbent. Fairly continuous flowering.
Yvonne Rabier	good in pots	3 × 2 ft (0.9 × 0.6 m)	Double. Polyantha.

YELLOW AND BUFF ROSES

Height 15 ft/4.5 m or more

Alister Stella Gray	**R,** *	15 × 10 ft (4.5 × 3.0 m)	Double, yolk fading to cream. Repeat-flowering.
Emily Gray	*	15 × 10 ft (4.5 × 3 m)	Double, golden yellow. Attractive foliage.

Lawrence Johnston	**Cl**, *	25 × 20 ft (7.6 × 6.0 m)	Semi-double, fine yellow. Early. Attractive foliage.
Mermaid	**Cl**, good on a north wall, *	30 × 25 ft (9.0 × 7,6 m)	Single. Fairly continuous flowering. One of the greats.

Height 8 ft/2.5 m to 15 ft/4.5 m

Gloire de Dijon	**Cl**, prone to blackspot but forgiven	12 × 8 ft (3.0 × 2.5 m)	Double, peachy buff. Repeat-flowering.
Golden Showers	**Cl**, good as a shrub, *	10 × 6 ft (3.0 × 1.8 m)	Double. Always in flower.
Goldfinch	**R**, weeping standard, *	8 × 5 ft (2.5 × 1.5 m)	Double, soft golden yellow. Attractive foliage.
Leverkusen	**Cl**, good as a shrub, *	10 × 8 ft (3.5 × 2.5 m)	Double. Fairly continuous flowering.
Rêve d'Or	**Cl**, good in pots	12 × 8 ft (3.6 × 2.5 m)	Double, soft buff. A bit tender. Repeat-flowering.

Height 4 ft/1.2 m to 8 ft/2.4 m

Agnes	**Sh**, hybrid Rugosa, *	6 × 5 ft (1.8 × 1.5 m)	Double, amber. Repeat-flowering.
Canary Bird	**Sh**, weeping standard, *	8 × 6 ft (2.5 × 1.8 m)	Single, no scent. Attractive foliage.
Chinatown	**Fl**, good in pots	5 × 3 ft (1.5 × 0.9 m)	Double, clear unfading yellow. Fairly continuous flowering.
Frühlingsgold	**Sh**, *	7 × 5 ft (2 × 1.5 m)	Single, prolific
Graham Thomas	**Sh**	4 × 4 ft (1.2 × 1.2 m)	Double, 'old-fashioned' flowers. Fairly continuous flowering.
R. headleyensis	**Sp**,*	7 × 5 ft (2 × 1.5 m)	Single, cream-yellow. Attractive foliage.
R. primula	**Sp**	5 × 4 ft (1.5 × 1.2 m)	Single. The Incense Rose. Attractive foliage.
Thisbe	**HM**,*	4 × 4 ft (1.2 × 1.2 m)	Double, straw-coloured flowers in clusters. Fairly continuous flowering.

Height 1 ft/0.3 m to 4 ft/1.2 m

Korresia	**Fl**, standard	2.5 × 2 ft (0.7 × 0.6 m)	Double, large unfading flowers. Fairly continuous flowering.
Yellow Cushion	**Fl**	2 × 2 ft (0.6 × 0.6 m)	Double, yellow fading to cream. Fairly continuous flowering. Bushy habit.

Height 15 ft/4.5 m or more

Desprez à Fleurs Jaunes	**Cl**	20 × 10 ft (7 × 3 m)	Double, quartered, soft orange-buff flowers. Repeat-flowering.
François Juranville	**R,** weeping standard,*	15 × 10 ft (4.5 × 3 m)	Double. A better 'Albertine'.

Height 8 ft/2.5 m to 15 ft/4.5 m

Alchemist	**Cl**	12 × 8 ft (3.6 × 2.5 m)	Double, full 'old-fashioned' yellow and orange flowers.
Aviateur Blériot	**R,** weeping standard	12 × 6 ft (3.6 × 1.8 m)	Double. Trusses of small, orange-yellow flowers fading to cream. Attractive foliage.
Compassion	**Cl**	10 × 6 ft (3 × 1.8 m)	Double, apricot-copper. Repeat-flowering. Attractive foliage.
Lady Hillingdon	**Cl,** good in pots, needs shelter	15 × 8 ft (4.5 × 2.5 m)	Double, apricot-yellow. Repeat-flowering.
Meg	**Cl**	8 × 4 ft (2.5 × 1.2 m)	Single, large, buff-apricot. Repeat-flowering. Attractive foliage.
Phyllis Bide	**R,** weeping standard, *	10 × 6 ft (3 × 1.8)	Semi-double, small pink-gold flowers in clusters. Fairly continuous flowering.

Height 4 ft/1.2 m to 8 ft/2.4 m

Buff Beauty	**HM,** standard, *	5 × 5 ft (1.5 × 1.5 m)	Double, aptly named. Fairly continuous flowering. Young leaves copper-red.
Charles Austin	**Sh**	5 × 4 ft (1.5 × 1.2 m)	Double, large 'old-fashioned' flowers.
Cornelia	**HM,** *	5 × 5 ft (1.5 × 1.5 m)	Double, pinky apricot. Fairly continuous flowering. Best in autumn.
Francesca	**HM,** good in pots, *	4 × 4 ft (1.2 × 1.2 m)	Single, flowers in large sprays. fairly continuous flowering. Attractive foliage.
Lady Penzance	**Sh,** *	7 × 6 ft (2 × 1.8 m)	Single, copper-pink. Foliage attractive and strongly scented. Hips.

Height 1 ft/0.3 m to 4 ft/1.2 m

Chanelle	**F1,** good in pots	3 × 2 ft (0.9 × 0.6 m)	Semi-double, very free-flowering.
Gruss an Aachen	good in pots	2 × 2 ft (0.6 × 0.6 m)	Double, palest apricot fading to white. Fairly continuous flowering.
Everest Double Fragrance	**Fl,** good in pots	4 × 3 ft (1.2 × 0.9 m)	Double, pale apricot pink. Fairly continuous flowering.

Mrs Oakley Fisher	**HT,** good in pots	3 × 3 ft (0.9 × 0.9 m)	Single, clear, soft orange. Fairly continuous flowering.
Perle d'Or	China, good in pots	4 × 2 ft (1.2 × 0.6 m)	Double. Small, delicate, pretty buds like 'Cécile Brunner'. Fairly continuous flowering.
Whisky Mac	**HT,** good in pots	3 × 2 ft (0.9 × 0.6 m)	Double, amber. Fairly continuous flowering. Attractive foliage.

ROSES WITH PINK FLOWERS

Height 15 ft/4.5 m and over

Kew Rambler	**R,** weeping standard, *	18 × 12 ft (5.4 × 3.6 m)	Single, rose-pink flowers in clusters. Grey-green leaves. Hips.
May Queen	**R,** weeping standard, ground cover, *	15 × 8 ft (4.5 × 2.5 m)	Semi-double, mauve-pink, in clusters. Attractive foliage.
Paul's Himalayan Musk	**Cl,** ground cover, *	20 × 12 ft (7 × 3.6 m)	Double, prolific small, soft pink flowers in clusters

Height 8 ft/2.5 m to 15 ft/4.5 m

Aloha	**Cl**	10 × 6 ft (3 × 1.8 m)	Double, lush, full flowers, rich pink. Strong. Fairly continuous flowering.
Blairii No. 2	**Cl**	12 × 8 ft (3.6 × 2.5 m)	Double, large full flowers. Repeat-flowering.
Cerise Bouquet	**Sh,** widely arching, *	12 × 12 ft (3.6 × 3.6 m)	Semi-double, Floriferous. Attractive foliage.
Complicata	**Sh,** spectacular as specimen, *	10 × 6 ft (3 × 1.8 m)	Single, bright pink.
Constance Spry	**Sh.** best as climber	20 × 10 ft (7 × 3 m)	Double, huge, opulent rose-pink.
Débutante	**R,** weeping standard	12 × 10 ft (3.6 × 3 m)	Double, small, soft rose-pink flowers in sprays. Attractive foliage.
Lady Sylvia	**Cl**	15 × 10 ft (4.5 × 3 m)	Double, rich flesh pink
Mme Grégoire Staechelin	**Cl,** robust	15 × 10 ft (4.5 × 3 m)	Double, huge flowers. Repeat-flowering. Attractive foliage and hips.
New Dawn	**Cl,** deservedly ubiquitous	10 × 8 ft (3 × 2.5 m)	Double. Fairly continuous flowering.

Height 4 ft/1.2 m to 8 ft/2.4 m

Bloomfield Abundance	**Sh,** good in pots	6 × 4 ft (1.8 × 1.2 m)	Double, prolific pale flesh-pink flowers (like 'Cécile Brunner' but more vigorous). Fairly continuous flowering.

176

Celestial	Alba, healthy and beautiful, *	6 × 4 ft (1.8 × 1.2 m)	Semi-double, softest pink. Attractive foliage.
Fantin-Latour	**Cent**, dense	5 × 4 ft (1.5 × 1.2 m)	Double, full, blush-pink.
Felicia	**HM**, good in pots, bushy	5 × 5 ft (1.5 × 1.5 m)	Double, silvery pink. Fairly continuous flowering.
Great Maiden's Blush	Alba, *	5 × 5 ft (1.5 × 1.5 m)	Double, palest flesh-pink. Attractive foliage.
Kazanlik	**Dam**, ancient rose, *	5 × 4 ft (1.5 × 1.2 m)	Double, strong scent. Repeat-flowering.
Königin von Danemark	Alba, *	5 × 5 ft (1.5 × 1.2 m)	Double, quartered pink flowers. Greyish leaves.
Lady Curzon	**Rug**, good in pots, spreading	4 × 6 ft (1.2 × 1.8 m)	Single, large wild-rose-pink flowers. Repeat-flowering.
Lavender Lassie	**HM**, *	5 × 4 ft (1.5 × 1.2 m)	Double, mauve-pink in large trusses. Fairly continuous flowering.
Marguerite Hilling	**Sh**	8 × 7 ft (2.5 × 2 m)	Single. Pink version of 'Nevada'. Repeat-flowering.
Mme Isaac Pereire	**Bourb**, *	7 × 5 ft (2 × 1.5 m)	Double, huge deep purplish-pink flower. Fairly continuous flowering.
Penelope	**HM**, good in pots	5 × 4 ft (1.5 × 1.2 m)	Semi-double palest cream-pink. Repeat-flowering.
Poulsen's Park Rose	**Sh**, *	6 × 6 ft (1.8 × 1.8 m)	Double, large silver-pink flowers. Repeat-flowering.
R. pomifera	**Sp**, *	6 × 5 ft (1.8 × 1.5 m)	Single. Huge round hips. Scented leaves.
R. rubrifolia	**Sp**, *	6 × 5 ft (1.8 × 1.5 m)	Single. Pinky-purpley-grey leaves. No scent.
R. virginiana	**Sp**, *	5 × 3 ft (1.5 × 1 m)	Single. Lasting hips. Autumn colour.
R. willmottiae	**Sp**, ground cover, good in pots	6 × 6 ft (1.8 × 1.8 m)	Single, mauve-pink flowers. Small pinkish-grey leaves.

Height 1 ft/0.3 m to 4 ft/1.2 m

Alfred de Dalmas (Mousseline)	Moss, good in pots	3 × 2 ft (1 × 0.6 m)	Semi-double. Very tidy and continuous flowering for a moss rose.
Baroness Rothschild	**HP**, good in pots	4 × 3 ft (1.2 × 1 m)	Double, huge soft pink flowers. Repeat-flowering.
Bonica	**Sh**, ground cover, good modern shrub	3 × 6 ft (1 × 1.8 m)	Semi-double. Fairly continuous flowering.
Comte de Chambord	**Port**	3 × 2 ft (1 × 0.6 m)	Double, lilac-pink full flowers. Fairly continuous flowering.

Empress Josephine (*R. × francofurtana*)	**Gall**, good in pots	4 × 3 ft (1.2 × 1 m)	Semi-double, large mid-pink, veined flowers. Little scent.
Frau Dagmar Hartopp	**Rug**, ground cover, good in pots, *	3 × 4 ft (1 × 1.2 m)	Single, clear pink flowers. Repeat-flowering. No scent. Fresh green leaves colouring autumn. Large crimson hips.
Grouse	**Sh**, ground cover, dense and sprawling, *	2 × 10 ft (0.6 × 3 m)	Single. Numerous small, pale pink flowers. No scent. Repeat-flowering.
Hermosa	**China**, good in pots	3 × 2 ft (1 × 0.6 m)	Double, delicate pale pink flowers. Repeat-flowering.
Ipsilante	**Gall**, good in pots	4 × 3 ft (1.2 × 1 m)	Double, large, quartered, lilac-pink flowers.
Ispahan	**Dam**	4 × 3 ft (1.2 × 1 m)	Semi-double, strong pink flowers. Good foliage.
Macrantha Raubritter	**Sh**, ground cover, dense and trailing, *	3 × 6 ft (1 × 1.8 m)	Semi-double, clear pink, cupped flowers.
Mary Rose	**Sh**, robust modern shrub, good in pots	4 × 4 ft (1.2 × 1.2 m)	Double, full, old-fashioned flowers. Fairly continuous flowering.
Max Graf	**Sh**, ground cover, dense and vigorous, *	1 × 8 ft (0.3 × 2.5 m)	Single flowers.
Mme Pierre Oger	**Bourb**, good in pots, prone to blackspot	4 × 4 ft (1.2 × 1.2 m)	Double, delicate, palest pink cupped flowers. Fairly continuous flowering.
Natalie Nypels	**Fl**, ground cover, good in pots	3 × 3 ft (1 × 1 m)	Double, rose-pink polyantha. Fairly continuous flowering.
Nozomi	**Sh**, weeping standard, ground cover, good in pots, *	1 × 6 ft (0.3 × .8 m)	Single, profuse, tiny, pale flowers.
Petite de Hollande	**Cent**, good in pots, neat	4 × 3 ft (1.2 × m)	Double.
Pompon de Bourgogne	**Cent**, standard, good in pots, compact and tidy	2 × 2 ft (0.6 × 0.6 m)	Double flowers.
The Fairy	standard, ground cover, good in pots, *	2 × 4 ft (0.6 × 1.2 m)	Double. Polyantha. Starts late and keeps going.
Yesterday	**Sh**, standard, ground cover, good in pots	4 × 4 ft (1.2 × 1.2 m)	Semi-double. Sprays of darkish mauve-pink little flowers.

Height 15 ft/4.5 m and over

Crimson Shower	**R,** weeping standard, ground cover	15 × 8 ft (4.5 × 2.5 m)	Double. No scent. Like 'Excelsa' but later, richer colour and less prone to mildew.

Height 8 ft/2.5 m to 15 ft/4.5 m

Anne of Geierstein	**Sh,** wild garden or hedge, *	10 × 8 ft (3 × 2.5 m)	Single flowers. Hybrid sweet briar with deep crimson flowers. Scented foliage. Hips.
Cerise Bouquet	**Sh,** graceful, arching, deserves space	12 × 12 ft (3.6 × 3.6 m)	Double flowers. Attractive foliage.
Cramoisi Supérieur	**Cl,** good in pots	12 × 8 ft (3.6 × 2.5 m)	Semi-double, strong unfading red flowers. Little scent.
Etoile d'Hollande	**Cl**	12 × 8 ft (3.6 × 2.5 m)	Double, rich, dark crimson HT.
Guinée	**Cl**	15 × 8 ft (4.5 × 2.5 m)	Double, darkest maroon-crimson HT. Opulent scent. Repeat-flowering.
Parkdirektor Riggers	**Cl,** *	10 × 6 ft (3 × 1.8 m)	Single, pure, strong red flowers in large clusters. Fairly continuous flowering.
Scarlet Fire	**Sh,** will also climb	10 × 6 ft (3 × 1.8 m)	Single flowers, well named.

Height 4 ft/1.2 m to 8 ft/2.4 m

Autumn fire (Herbstfeuer)	**Sh,** *	6 × 8 ft (1.8 × 2.5 m)	Semi-double, large blood-red. Fine hips.
Fiona	**Sh,** ground cover	4 × 6 ft (1.2 × 1.8 m)	Semi-double, plentiful, blood-red. No scent. Fairly continuous flowering.
Fountain	**Sh,** good in pots, healthy, *	5 × 4 ft (1.5 × 1.2 m)	Double, large, crimson-red. Dark green foliage. Fairly continuous flowering.
James Mason	**Sh,** good in pots	5 × 4 ft (1.5 × 1.2 m)	Semi-double, crimson. Golden antlers.
Nur Mahal	**HM,** *	4 × 5 ft (1.2 × 1.5 m)	Semi-double, light crimson flowers in clusters. Healthy, dark green foliage.

Height 1 ft/0.3 m to 4 ft/1.2 m

Dusky Maiden	**Fl,** bushy	2 × 2 ft (0.6 × 0.6 m)	Single, dusky crimson velvet. Fairly continuous flowering.
Evelyn Fison	**Fl,** healthy	2.5 × 2 ft (0.7 × 0.6 m)	Double, bright scarlet.

Europeana	**Fl**	2.5 × 2 ft (0.7 × 0.6 m)	Double, deep crimson. Bronze leaves. Fairly continuous flowering.
Red Bells	**Sh**, neat, ground cover, good in pots	2 × 4 ft (0.6 × 1.2 m)	Double, small flowers in clusters. Good foliage. Fairly continuous flowering.
Rosa gallica officinalis	**Gall**, good in pots, ancient rose, *	3 × 3 ft (1 × 1 m)	Semi-double flowers. The Apothecary's Rose.
Rose de Rescht	good in pots	3 × 2 ft (1 × 0.6 m)	Very double, small pompoms. Repeat-flowering.

PURPLE AND MAUVE ROSES

Height 15 ft/4.5 m and over

Rose Marie Viaud	**R**, arching shrub or will climb a tree, *	15 × 8 ft (4.5 × 2.5 m)	Double, purple fading to pale lilac. No scent.
Veilchenblau	**R**, *	15 × 12 ft (4.5 × 3.6 m)	Semi-double, early flowers. Fade less if grown in shade.
Violette	**R**, thornless, *	15 × 10 ft (4.5 × 3 m)	Double, early flowers, crimson-purple fading to grey-mauve.

Height 8 ft/2.5 m to 15 ft/4.5 m

Amadis	**R**, thornless	10 × 6 ft (3 × 1.8 m)	Double. Earliest purple rambler. No scent.
Bleu Magenta	**R**, *	12 × 10 ft (3.6 × 3 m)	Double, almost true violet. Largest of the purples. Late flowering.

Height 4 ft/1.2 m to 8 ft/2.4 m

Belle de Crécy	**Gall**, good in pots, floppy	4 × 3 ft (1.2 × 1 m)	Double flowers, starting strong pink and fading through violet to soft mauve-grey.
Capitaine John Ingram	**Moss**, tidy, dense bush	6 × 4 ft (1.8 × 1.2 m)	Double, dark purple crimson flowers. Reddish moss.
Cardinal de Richelieu	**Gall**, good in pots	4 × 3 ft (1.2 × 1 m)	Double, rich velvet purple.
Charles de Mills	**Gall**, dense compact shrub	4 × 3 ft (1.2 × 1 m)	Double, large, very full quartered flowers of rich, dark red-purple. Long flowering period. Little scent.
Duc de Guiche	**Gall**, sprawls	4 × 4 ft (.2 × 1.2 m)	Double, crimson magenta flowers with green eye. Highly scented.
Gipsy Boy (Zigeuner Knabe)	**Sh**, robust shrub for poor soils, *	6 × 4 ft (1.8 × 1.2 m)	Double, black-crimson.

Jeanne Duval	**Gall,** good in pots	4 × 3 ft (1.2 × 1 m)	Double flowers, each pink, magenta lavender and grey. Scented.
Reine de Violettes	**HP**	5 × 3 ft (1.5 × 1 m)	Double, soft violet flowers set off greyish leaves. Fairly continuous flowering.
Scabrosa	**Rug,** robust, *	6 × 4 ft (1.8 × 1.2 m)	Single, huge, crimson-mauve flowers. No scent. Huge, red hips. Repeat-flowering.
Tuscany Superb	**Gall,** good in pots	4 × 3 ft (1.2 × 1 m)	Semi-double, large, black-crimson flowers.

Height 1 ft/0.3 m to 4 ft/2.4 m

Cardinal Hume	**Sh**	3 × 3.5 ft (1 × 1.06 m)	Double, red-purple flowers in clusters. Repeat flowering.
Cosimo Ridolfi	**Gall,** good in pots	3 × 3 ft (1 × 1 m)	Double, soft mauve-grey flowers held upright. Grey-green leaves.
Escapade	**Fl,** good in pots, *	4 × 3 ft (1.2 × 1 m)	Single, plentiful lavender-pink flowers. Fairly continuous flowering.
Lilac Charm	**Fl,** good in pots, neat and bushy	2 × 2 ft (0.6 × 0.6 m)	Single. Free flowering.
Robert le Diable	**Cent,** good in pots, sprawls	3 × 3 ft (1 × 1 m)	Double, late flowers with subtle depth of mixed colours.

STRIPED ROSES

Height 4 ft/1.2 m to 8 ft/2.4 m

Commandant Beaurepaire	**Bourb,** good as climber, black-spot on poor soil	6 × 5 ft (1.8 × 1.5 m)	Double, cream flowers with purple stripes. Sparse foliage – fairly continuous flowering.
Ferdinand Pichard	**HP**	5 × 4 ft (1.5 × 1.2 m)	Double, pink flowers striped crimson and purple. Fairly continuous flowering.
Variegata di Bologna	**Bourb,** good as climber, black-spot on poor soil	6 × 5 ft (1.8 × 1.5 m)	Double, cream flowers with purple stripes. Sparse foliage.

Height 1 ft/0.3 m to 4 ft/1.2 m

Camaieux	**Gall,** good in pots, weak growth	3 × 3 ft (1 × 1 m)	Double, white flowers with crimson-purple stripes which fade to grey.
Rosa Mundi (R. gallica *versicolor*)	**Gall,** good in pots, excellent healthy shrub, ancient, *	3 × 3 ft (1 × 1 m)	Semi-double, large, light crimson flowers splashed with pale pink and white. Attractive foliage.

Complementary Plants

BACKGROUND PLANTING

Formal hedging and informal foliage shrubs:

Evergreens

Box (*Buxus sempervirens*)
Holly (*Ilex aquifolium*)
Pittosporum tenuifolium
Portugal laurel (*Prunus lusitanica*)
Sea buckthorn (*Hippophae rhamnoides*)
Yew (*Taxus baccata*)

Deciduous green

Beech
Field maple
Hornbeam
Pleached lime
Quickthorn (Hawthorn)
Sweet briar (*Rosa rubiginosa*)

Deciduous red/purple

Berberis thunbergii 'Atropurpurea' or 'Red Chief'
Corylus maxima 'Purpurea'
Cotinus coggyria 'Foliis purpureis'
Malus eleyi
Prunus cistena 'Crimson Dwarf'
Prunus pissardii 'Nigra'
Purple beech
Rosa glauca (R. *rubrifolia*)

Background shrubs to flower before roses (*evergreen):

Late Winter

Camellia japonica
Chaenomeles
Lonicera fragrantissima

Viburnum x *bodnantense*
Viburnum farreri (*fragrans*)
**Viburnum tinus*

Spring

Amelanchier
**Osmanthus* x *burkwoodii*
**Osmanthus delavayi*
**Prunus laurocerasus*
Ribes alpinum
Ribes odoratum
Spiraea x *arguta*
Spiraea thunbergii
**Viburnum burkwoodii*
Viburnum carlesii
Viburnum juddii

Early summer

**Ceanothus*
**Choisya ternata*
Cytisus multiflorus
Cytisus praecox
Deutzia rosea 'Campanulata'
Halesia carolina
Kolkwitzia amabilis
Paeonia delavayi
Paeonia lutea ludlowii
Poncirus trifoliata
Sambucus (various)
Syringa
Viburnum lantana
Viburnum plicatum 'Lanarth' and 'Mariesii'
**Viburnum rhytidophyllum*
Weigela middendorffiana

Shrubs to flower after roses (from late summer):

**Abelia* x *grandiflora*

**Arbutus unedo*
Buddleias
Ceanothus 'Gloire de Versailles' and 'Topaz'
Deutzia monbeigii
**Elaeagnus ebbingei*
**Escallonias*
Genista aetnensis
Hydrangeas
**Itea ilicifolia*
**Ligustrum japonicum*
**Ligustrum lucidum*
Spartium junceum
Spiraea x *bumalda* 'Anthony Waterer'

FOREGROUND PLANTING

Formal edging, clipped

Berberis thunbergii 'Atropurpurea Nana'
**Buxus sempervirens*
**Hebe anomala* (white flowers late summer)
**Lavandula* 'Hidcote'
**Lavandula* 'Loddon Pink'
**Lavandula* 'Munstead Dwarf'
**Lavandula* 'Nana Alba'
**Rosmarinus officinalis*
**Salvia officinalis*
**Salvia officinalis* 'Purpurascens'
**Santolina chamaecyparissus* 'Nana'
**Santolina virens*
**Teucrium chamaedrys*

Informal edging

Any of the above, left untrimmed.

Grey foliage 1–2 ft/0·3–0·6 m

Achillea clypeolata, A. 'Moon-
    shine'
Anaphalis triplinervis
*Anthemis cupaniana
Artemisia canescens, A. stelleriana
*Ballota pseudodictamnus
Caryopteris x clandonensis 'Kew
    Blue'
Codonopsis clematidea
Crambe maritima
*Dianthus Highland Hybrids and
    other pinks
Dicentra formosa 'Adrian Bloom'
*Dorycnium hirsutum
Eryngium bourgatii, E. maritinum
Geranium renardii
Gypsophila paniculata 'Rosy Veil'
*Hebe albicans, *H. pinguifolia
    'Pagei'
Hosta fortunei hyacinthina, H.
    sieboldiana 'Elegans'
Lychnis coronaria, L. coronaria
    'Alba'
Nepeta mussinii
*Ruta graveolens 'Jackman's Blue'
*Santolina neapolitana
Scabiosa graminifolia
Sedum 'Autumn Joy', S. spectabile

Green foliage 1–2 ft/0·3–0·6 m

Alchemilla mollis
*Armeria plantaginea
Aster thomsonii 'Nanus'
*Bergenia (many varieties)
Campanula alliarifolia, C. 'Burgh-
    altii', C. carpatica
Chrysanthemum parthenium
Cytisus x beanii, C. x kewensis, C.
    purpureus
Euphorbia dulcis, E. polychroma
Geraniums (most varieties)
*Hebe 'Autumn Glory', *H. x fran-
    ciscana 'Blue Gem', *H. raka-
    ensis

Helleborus (most varieties)
*Heuchera x brizoides
x Heucherella tiarelloides
Hostas (most varieties)
Hyssopus officinalis
Oenothera tetragona
Penstemons
Platycodon grandiflorus
Salvia × superba 'May Night'
*Santolina virens
Schizostylis coccinea
Sisyrinchium striatum
Viola cornuta

Grey foliage under 1 ft/0·3 m

Acaena adscendens, A. caesii-
    glauca, A. inermis
*Alyssum saxatile
Aubrieta
*Dianthus
Dicentra oregona
Euphorbia myrsinites
Helianthemum 'Wisley Pink', H.
    'Wisley Primrose' and some
    others
Stachys lanata (S. olympica)
*Thymus languinosus
Veronica incana

Green foliage under 1 ft/0·3 m

Alchemilla conjuncta
Anthemis nobilis
*Armeria maritima
Campanula portenschlagiana (C.
    muralis)
Chives
*Fragaria vesca
Helianthemums, various
Iberis
*Lamium maculatum
Parsley
Phlox (alpine varieties)
Pulsatilla vulgaris
*Thymus
Vinca minor
*Viola cornuta, *V. labradorica
    (purple foliage) and others

Yellow foliage under 1 ft/0·3 m

Origanum vulgare 'Aureum'
*Thymus x citriodorus 'Aureus'

GROUND COVER UNDER ROSES

The following plants will carpet
the ground without competing
with the roses.

Acaena
*Ajuga reptans 'Atropurpurea'
Aubrieta
Brunnera macrophylla
Convallaria majalis
Corydalis ochroleuca
Cyclamen hederifolium (C. nea-
    politanum)
Dicentra formosa varieties
Fragaria vesca
*Lamium maculatum 'Aureum'
*Lysimachia nummularia 'Aurea'
Omphalodes cappadocica
*Oxalis oregana
Primula auricula
*Pulmonaria
*Saxifraga umbrosa and mossy
    saxifrages
*Tiarella cordifolia
*Vinca minor
*Viola labradorica
*Viola odorata

Spring bulbs are effective planted
under roses, either with ground
cover plants or alone, e.g.
Anemone blanda, Chionodoxa,
Crocus, Fritillaria, Galanthus,
Muscari, dwarf Narcissus, Scilla,
species Tulips.

INTERPLANTING AMONG ROSES:

FORM

Spikey leaves or flowers

Acanthus
Campanula, several
Cimifuga cordifolia, C. racemosa
Crocosmia
Delphinium
Digitalis
Hemerocallis
Iris germanica, I. sibirica
Libertia formosa
Lupins
Phormium
Polygonum bistorta 'Superbum'
Salvia × superba
Schizostylis
Sisyrinchium striatum
Verbascums
Veronicas
Yuccas

Dome-shaped plants

Buxus sempervirens (clipped)
Ceanothus thyrsiflorus 'Repens'
Choisya ternata
Cistus
Euphorbia, several
Geranium (many varieties)
Hebe (many)
Ilex aquifolium (clipped)
Lavandula
Lonicera nitida 'Baggesen's Gold'
Olearia × haastii
Osmanthus delavayi
Potentilla fruticosa (most varieties)
Rosmarinus
Ruta graveolens
Salvia officinalis
Santolina
Senecio 'Sunshine'

Bold foliage

Acanthus
Anemone x hybrida
Angelica archangelica
Bergenia
Brunnera
Catalpa bignonioides 'Aurea'
Crambe cordifolia
Cynara cardunculus
Euphorbia characias wulfenii
Hostas
Hydrangea sargentiana
Peonies (several)
Verbascum

COLOUR

Blues and lavenders

Abutilon vitifolium (wall shrub)
Aquilegia 'McKana Hybrids'
Baptisia australis
Buddleia alternifolia 'Argentea'
Campanula, several
Clematis, several
Eryngium alpinum
Geranium, several
Iris, many varieties
Lavandula
Linaria purpurea (toadflax)
Nepeta, several
Platycodon grandiflorum
Polemonium caeruleum
Pulsatilla vulgaris
Salvia haematodes, S. superba
Thalictrum aquilegifolium

Pink, red, purple

Aquilegia 'Norah Barlow'
Armeria maritima
Campanula lactiflora 'Loddon Anna'
Cistus 'Silver Pink'
Clematis, several
Dianthus, many varieties
Deutzia, several
Geranium, several

Gypsophila 'Rosy Veil'
Helianthemum, many varieties
Heuchera, all varieties
Iris germanica, several
Phlomis italica
Potentilla 'The Princess'
Saxifraga umbrosa
Verbascum 'Pink Domino'
Weigela, all varieties

Yellow and lime

Achillea
Alchemilla mollis
Asphodeline luteus
Catalpa bignonioides 'Aurea'
Cytisus battandieri
Digitalis grandiflora (D. ambigua)
Eremurus bungei
Euphorbia myrsinites
Genista lydia
Gleditsia triacanthos 'Sunburst'
Helianthemum (several)
Hemerocallis (several)
Ligustrum ovalifolium 'Aureum'
Lonicera nitida 'Baggesen's Gold'
Oenothera missouriensis
Philadelphus coronarius 'Aureus'
Phlomis fruticosa
Potentilla fruticosa
Sisyrinchium striatum
Spartium junceum
Spiraea 'Goldmound'

White

Clematis 'Marie Boisselot'
Cytisus albus
Delphinium 'Galahad'
Deutzia (several)
Dicentra spectabilis 'Alba'
Exochorda macrantha
Hebe albicans (and others)
Libertia formosa
Lilium regale, L. candidum
Lupins
Lychnis coronaria 'Alba'
Papaver 'Perry's White'
Polemonium caeruleum 'Album'

Rose Gardens to Visit

The following lists give a selection of rose gardens or gardens where roses dominate in summer time. I have visited most of those in the United Kingdom and some in France. For other countries, I am indebted to the World Federation of Rose Societies for information.

Lack of space prevents me from listing many other remarkable gardens from all over the world.

ENGLAND

For opening times refer to the 'Yellow Book', *Gardens of England and Wales* or to *Historic Houses, Castles and Gardens*.

THE SOUTH

Hampshire

57 Church Road, Bramshott.
Writer and rose expert Hazel le Rougetel's tiny garden full of roses. Visit by appointment only.

Broadhatch House, Bentley.
Climbers, Species and old shrub roses. Circular, yew-hedged sunken garden of Hybrid Musks. Interesting background shrubs and interplanting throughout.

Fairfield House, Hambledon.
Many unusual shrub and climbing roses on chalk. Species and shrub roses grown free-standing in grass. Fine hips in autumn.

Greatham Mill, Liss.
Mature garden, well-designed for form and colour with many rare plants. Roses dominate in summer.

Jenkyn Place, Bentley.
Famous garden with distinguished collection of trees and shrubs, including many species, shrub and climbing roses. Formal enclosed garden of H.T. and Species roses with central pool. Tiny garden of old roses behind 'Rosa Mundi' hedge.

Mottisfont Abbey.
Designed by Graham Stuart Thomas for the National Trust's collection of old roses. Essential place of pilgrimage for rose lovers.

West Green House, Hartley Wintney.
National Trust. Wild and romantic.

Kent

Brewhouse, Boughton Aluph.
Small, plantsman's garden. Old roses skilfully trained (pegged down).

Goodnestone Park.
See pages 165–7.

Hartlip Place, Sittingbourne.
Secret garden of shrub roses with formal layout within larger $3\frac{3}{4}$ acre garden.

Hever Castle, Edenbridge.
Formal, enclosed by fine, arched brick walls, planted with massed 'Iceberg' and other Floribunda and H.T. roses.

Mount Ephraim, Hernhill.
Formal rose terraces above fine gardens.

Penshurst Place.
Climbing roses on every wall, rose pergola in the Nut Garden, and several rose gardens.

The Old Parsonage, Sutton Valence.
Fine climbing and shrub roses contribute to mixed planting with emphasis on ground cover.

Saltwood Castle, Hythe.
Roses spilling from castle walls.

Scotney Castle.
Roses surround romantic castle ruins. National Trust.

Sissinghurst Castle.
Roses everywhere in June and July in Vita Sackville-West's famous garden, now owned by the National Trust.

Greater London
Hampton Court Palace,
Kew Gardens and
Queen Mary's Rose Garden,
Regent's Park.
Fine displays of modern roses massed on a grand scale. Kew also has a collection planted to demonstrate the history of the rose.

Highwood Ash, Highwood Hill, NW7.
Small, formal, enclosed garden with 14 rose beds. Part of $3\frac{1}{4}$ acre garden.

Surrey
Busbridge Wood, Munstead.
One fifth acre formal, yew-hedged rose garden paved in York stone, laid out in 1946 by Percy Cane part of his plan for the $10\frac{1}{2}$ acre grounds.

Haslehurst, Haslemere.
Formal, paved, enclosed rose garden with central pond and fountain laid out in 1892 by rose-breeding friend of Gertrude Jekyll.

High Meadow, Churt.
One acre with all kinds of roses, including David Austin's English Roses, used in informal, colour-planned, mixed borders.

Polesden Lacey, Bookham.
National Trust. Typical Edwardian rose garden of a grand country house.

Wisley.
The Royal Horticultural Society's gardens include displays of all kinds of roses including climbers on rope swags and 'ground cover' roses.

Sussex
Bakers Farm, Shipley.
New rosary planted in 1987. Roses interplanted with double white tulips.

Bateman's, Burwash.
National Trust. Rose garden made by Rudyard Kipling in 1906. Curved beds interlocking with pool and fountain; edgings of London pride and mossy saxifrage.

Casters Brook, Cocking.
Informal garden in old orchard with many old roses.

Charleston Manor, West Dean.
Fine collection of old roses in the walled gardens of a beautiful house.

Clinton Lodge, Fletching.
Formal, yew-hedged garden of exuberant old roses underplanted with *Alchemilla mollis*.

Ketches, Newick.
Massed plantings of shrub roses, ramblers growing into trees.

Nymans, Handcross.
National Trust. Arches and pillars in the French style support climbers. A wishing well is surrounded by old roses, others brought from French and Italian gardens early this century.

Isle of Wight
Little North Court, Shorwell.
Sunken garden surrounding lily pond, rose beds edged with pinks, pansies and auriculas.

Ningwood Manor, Newport.
Formal Victorian layout of circular and curved beds surrounded by hedges. Climbers and ramblers trained on pillars. Roses interplanted with shrubs and herbaceous plants.

CENTRAL ENGLAND

Bedfordshire
Luton Hoo, Luton.
Formal, Italianate, stone-paved, sunken rose garden with pond and fountain and 3,400 H.T. roses in soft colours, in box-edged beds.

Berkshire
Basildon Park, near Reading.
National Trust. Pretty, private rose garden, open occasionally, of old roses with other old-fashioned plants.

Chieveley Manor, Newbury.
Many kinds of roses in informal planting in red brick walled garden.

Folly Farm, Sulhamstead.
Lutyens/Jekyll layout with sunken rose garden.

Hazelby House, North End.
Climbers and old and modern shrub roses grow in yew-enclosed garden with unusual and rare herbaceous plants and small shrubs. Roses grow through Chinese style pergolas.

Littlecote, Hungerford.
The ultimate rose parterre, a new rose garden adjoining the restaurant with 4,000 bedding roses planted in a flower pattern in three 90 ft circles.

The Old Rectory, Burghfield.
Romantic, exuberantly planted garden with roses everywhere, especially climbers.

Buckinghamshire
Cliveden, Taplow.
National Trust. The rose garden in a wood was laid out for Lord and Lady Astor by Sir Geoffrey Jellicoe in 1959. Irregular beds in flowing shapes are linked by grey-blue wooden arches of elegant simplicity.

Great Barfield, Bradenham.
Species and shrub roses, many unusual, among other shrubs and growing into trees.

Hambleden Manor, Henley-on-Thames.
Hidden behind a high, rose-clad brick wall, romantically luxuriant plantings of old roses on chalk soil, richly coloured and bursting out of formal beds. Pretty rose arbour. Laid out by Peter Beales for Lady Hambleden in 1981.

Winslow Hall, Winslow.
Both formal and informal beds of roses in 3-acre garden of house designed by Wren.

Hertfordshire
Capel Manor, Waltham Cross.
In the old walled garden of this Horticultural and Environmental Centre, old roses are planted to demonstrate the history of their introduction.

Hatfield House, Hatfield.
Many roses throughout lovely gardens created by the Marchioness of Salisbury in keeping with historic Tudor and Jacobean house. Sweet briar hedges, old roses planted with herbs, Hybrid Musks and new English Roses.

Knebworth House, Knebworth.
Formal beds of Floribundas and Hybrid Teas, edged with box, in gardens laid out in 1840s.

The Gardens of the Rose, St Albans.
The Royal National Rose Society's display and trial gardens: 30,000 roses of every type in 12 acres. Old roses, pergolas, rope swags, bedding, ground cover, etc.

Oxfordshire
Brook Cottage, Alkerton.
Roses throughout informal 4-acre garden with well-planned colour schemes. Good display of shrub roses on grass bank.

Broughton Castle, Banbury.
One-quarter acre of box-edged rose beds laid out in 1880. Climbers, ramblers, old and modern shrub roses and Floribundas interplanted with agapanthus, phlox, salvias and santolina.

Pusey House, Faringdon.
The walled 'Lady Emily's Garden' has formal rose beds and a frame supporting climbing roses and clematis. Near the house are beds of old shrub roses, some rare, underplanted with choice ground cover plants including roses.

WEST MIDLANDS

Gloucestershire
Alderley Grange, Wotton under Edge.
Luxuriant groups of old roses, many rare, set off by carefully chosen herb plants and architectural topiary.

Hunts Court, Dursley.
Species and shrub roses, some rare, interplanted with unusual shrubs chosen for their foliage.

Kiftsgate Court, Chipping Campden.
Home of the biggest rose, *R. filipes* 'Kiftsgate'. Luxuriantly informal planting in formal framework makes much use of old and modern roses. Twin hedges of 'Rosa Mundi'. Good colour schemes and planting.

Sudeley Castle, Winchcombe.
See pages 155–8.

Shropshire
David Austin Roses, Albrighton.
Display gardens of nurseries specialising in old, Species, climbing and shrub roses. Home of the English breed of roses.

Hatton Grange, Shifnal.
Formal, enclosed garden of old roses. Fine climbers.

Warwickshire
Ivy Lodge, Radway.
Four-acre garden made in the last 30 years on the site of the Battle of Edgehill. Ebullient shrub, Species and climbing roses everywhere, specially up trees.

Ryton Gardens, the National
Centre for Organic Gardening,
near **Coventry**.
Formal, enclosed garden dem-
onstrates rose varieties that are
resistant to mildew and blackspot.

Warwick Castle.
See pages 47–8.

THE WEST

Avon

Abbots Leigh House, near Bristol.
Pretty, formal layout dating from
1936.

**The Little Manor, Farrington
Gurney.**
Secret, walled garden, rose beds
edged with aubrieta and underplanted with pansies and tulips.

Cornwall

Bosvigo House, Truro.
Many old roses in a series of walled
gardens and in woodland garden.

Devon

Bundels, Sidbury.
Three-quarter-acre cottage garden
full of scented roses. Hybrid Musk
hedge, arches and profuse, well-
chosen interplanting.

**Rosemoor Garden Charitable
Trust, Great Torrington.**
Lady Anne Palmer's garden, made
in the last thirty years, is full of
rare and interesting plants.

The Glebe House, Whitestone.
Two acres of lawns, trees and
climbing, shrub and Species roses
on a south-facing slope with views
to Dartmoor and the sea.

Dorset

Chilcombe House, Bridport.
See pages 168–70.

Cranborne Manor, Cranborne.
Lovely historic gardens first laid
out by John Tradescant in the 17th
century. Roses everywhere, as
shrubs, on walls, on a pergola,
along the Church Walk and in the
kitchen garden.

Steeple Manor, Steeple.
Laid out by Brenda Colvin in the
1920s round a pretty 16th/17th
century house, the recently
restored gardens are planted with
many interesting old roses, including climbers and beds of massed
Hybrid Musks.

**The Manor House, Hinton St
Mary.**
Beautiful 17th century house and
earlier tithe barn in 5 acres. Sunken
garden, stone walled and paved
with a large pool and raised beds
of Hybrid Tea and Floribunda
roses. Elsewhere Hybrid Musk and
Species roses in bold groups.

Somerset

Clapton Court, Crewkerne.
A small, formal pattern of beds
enclosed by yew and hornbeam
hedges, planted in red, white and
pink roses. More roses in shrubberies and woodland garden.

East End Farm, Pitney.
See pages 144–5.

**Hestercombe House, near
Taunton.**
Lutyens/Jekyll gardens carefully
restored by Somerset County
Council include a rose pergola and
a narrow garden of old roses with
central rill and elm arbour.

**Wootton House, near
Glastonbury.**
Gardens laid out by Avray Tipping
in the 1920s. Formal rose garden
adjoining house, many roses in
beds and on walls throughout
gardens.

Wiltshire

Andover House, Charlton Park.
See pages 159–60.

Balcony House, Sherston.
Small enclosed garden with formal
layout and romantically profuse
planting.

Bowood House, Calne.
Spectacular formal terraces of
roses interplanted with *Galtonia
candicans* link the Earl of Shel-
burne's fine Adam mansion to the
lovely park laid out by Capability
Brown.

Corsley Mill, near Warminster.
'Young' garden with formal framework to show distinguished collection of roses, some rare and
some bred by the owners. Interplanted with carefully chosen
shrubs and herbaceous plants, and
planned to keep the orange-yellow
colours separate from the pinky-
mauve. Small nursery.

**Fitz House, Teffont Magna, near
Salisbury.**
Four acres of shrubs and herbaceous plants mixed with roses
of all types including weeping standards and ramblers on arches.

Kellaways, near Chippenham.
Two and a half acres of roses thriving with other shrubs and herbaceous plants, many rare.

Sheldon Manor, Chippenham.
A series of enclosures and vistas, formally structured but informally planted, covers 8 acres around a medieval manor house. Species roses and old and modern shrub roses grow in borders and free-standing in grass; orchard trees are smothered in ramblers and climbers. Many rare varieties.

THE MIDLANDS

Leicestershire and Rutland

Arthingworth Manor, Market Harborough.
Winding paths between large beds of boldly grouped shrub roses, including some species grafted as double height standards. Ramblers as ground cover with self-seeded foxgloves and pansies.

Rockingham Castle, Market Harborough.
The gardens include the Cross, designed by John Codrington in 1910 for Mrs Wentworth Watson, planted with the pink Floribunda 'Pernille Poulsen' in beds edged with lavender and catmint. There is also a walk lined with standard roses and a circular rose garden dating from about 1820.

Whatton House, near Loughborough.
Whatton, famous for its fantastic Chinese Garden, also has two Edwardian rose gardens of great charm.

Lincolnshire

Doddington Hall, Lincoln.
The west, walled garden was laid out in 1900, with help from Kew, to be in keeping with the unspoilt Elizabethan mansion. Box-edged parterre beds hold roses and flag irises. Climbing roses on walls and Species and shrub roses in the wild garden.

Grimsthorpe Castle, Bourne.
A box-edged knot garden on the east front of the castle is filled with Floribunda roses and lavender, and on the west side there is a 70 yard border of old shrub roses.

Gunby Hall, Burgh-la-Marsh.
The walled gardens of Tennyson's 'Haunt of Ancient Peace' include rose beds edged with box and lavender and interplanted with hardy geraniums and ferns. More roses throughout the gardens.

The Manor House, Bitchfield.
One and a half acres laid out in 1970 with help from Robin Lane Fox; a long border divided by yew buttresses combines roses with other flowering shrubs and perennials in well-planned colour schemes.

Northamptonshire

Coton Manor, near Northampton.
Flanked by the 1662 house and old holly and yew hedges, the planting of old and modern roses is informal.

Nottinghamshire

Brewery House Cottage, Gamston.
Every inch of space in this informal cottage garden is used to achieve romantic luxuriance with shrub roses and other plants of distinction chosen particularly for their foliage.

Green Mile, Retford.
There are two formal, yew-hedged rose gardens and shrub roses in bold clumps in the wild garden.

Holme Pierrepont Hall, Radcliffe-on-Trent.
The courtyard of this medieval house was laid out as a parterre in 1875, perhaps designed by Nesfield. It was, and still is, flanked by simple rose beds, and climbers planted in the 1920s are still thriving.

Newstead Abbey, Linby.
Lord Byron's family home, now owned by Nottingham City Council, has extensive, well-kept gardens including a traditional walled rose garden with formal beds of modern roses around a central fountain, standards and weeping standards and a collection of old shrub roses.

Staffordshire

Roses du Temps Passé, Woodlands House, Stretton.
Garden designed by the author for nursery specialising in old roses has formal beds edged with santolina, arches, weeping standards and half-standards. Informal groups of Rugosa, Alba and Species roses surround informal pond.

Shugborough, Stafford.
A small part of the extensive pleasure gardens, the 'Victorian' rose garden was laid out by Graham Stuart Thomas in 1966 to a symmetrical design with arches and pillars to support climbers and ramblers.

THE NORTH

Cheshire

Arley Hall, Knutsford.
A fine collection of old shrub roses and Species rose in the rose garden by the Tea Cottage; fine clumps of Hybrid Musks at the entrances to the walled garden, an unusual and bold grouping of roses of different shades of red, and a quiet little enclosed garden of Hybrid Tea and Floribunda roses with lavender, known as the Flag Garden.

Cholmondley Castle, Malpas.
Double borders with big groups of 'Penelope', 'Felicia' and others lead into the formal, paved rose garden. Crossed arches form rose arbours and climbers hide the tennis court.

Poever Hall, Knutsford.
There are many roses throughout the gardens of the attractive Elizabethan house, and a formal rose garden of 10 beds enclosed by yew hedges in which windows have been cut to give glimpses to and from the adjoining herb garden. Old roses, including many striped, are underplanted with violas.

Cumbria

Holker Hall, Cark-in-Cartmel.
A secret, paved garden planned by Thomas Mawson in 1912, is approached by a curving pergola. This garden was replanted in 1988 with old roses for opulent colour and scent and lavish interplanting.

Derbyshire

Haddon Hall, Bakewell.
See pages 146–9.

Radburne Hall, Kirk Langley.
Beautiful Palladian house has immaculate terraces of Hybrid Tea roses from which there are fine views.

County Durham

Westholme Hall, Winston.
Enclosed formal rose garden within larger garden. Informally planted with old roses and well-chosen herbs and other perennials. Arches, pergola.

Merseyside

Windle Hall, St Helens.
Walled garden amidst woodland holds varied and colourful collection, mostly Hybrid Teas and Floribundas.

Yorkshire

Castle Howard, York.
The most comprehensive and best displayed collection of roses in Britain. There are four separate gardens, each different in style. Bowers, pergola, trellised pyramids and edgings and interplantings all noteworthy.

Newby Hall, Ripon.
Lavender-edged double beds of York and Lancaster roses and striped 'Rosa Mundi' represent 'The Wars of the Roses'. Handsome arched pergola. The sunken rose garden is a masterpiece.

Ripley Castle, Harrogate.
Surrounded by brick walls, the roses are interplanted with delphiniums and peonies, making a soft colour scheme of pinks, blues and white.

St Nicholas, Richmond.
A series of romantic, secret gardens with thickets of old shrub roses, tree peonies and philadelphus interplanted with foxgloves, columbines, cranesbills, martagon lilies and Japanese anemones.

Sledmere House, Driffield.
All kinds of roses, specially climbers, in walled garden, underplanted with polyanthus.

Sleightholme Dale, Kirbymoorside.
All types of roses in a walled garden with arches, pergola and pillars, interplanted with lavender, peonies, verbascums and sweet williams. More roses elsewhere in the garden.

Sutton Park, Sutton-on-the-Forest.
Terraces laid out by Percy Cane with formal, symmetrically arranged rose beds, now planted with Species and shrub roses.

The Dower House, Thirkleby.
Mostly old roses, triumphing over hostile environment: east wind, heavy clay and frost pocket.

EAST ANGLIA

Cambridgeshire

Duxford Mill, Duxford.
See pages 150–2.

Elton Hall, Peterborough.
Formal beds in the Victorian style laid out for the owners by Peter Beales in 1984 and planted with old roses chosen particularly for their scent. Over 1,000 roses, many unusual and rare.

Essex

Hyde Hall, Rettendon.
A large garden with a great many roses (4,500) well maintained and displayed in carefully planned colour schemes. The Rope Walk runs between climbers and ramblers trained on rope swags.

Norfolk

Mannington Hall, Saxthorpe.
The gardens surrounding the medieval house include many roses of all types. A 'Heritage Rose Garden' shows the evolution of rose garden styles from the Middle Ages.

Park House, Old Hunstanton.
Many roses throughout $3\frac{1}{2}$ acre garden, specially in old walled garden.

Wretham Lodge, East Wretham.
Species and shrub roses interplanted with hardy geraniums, hemerocallis, alliums, verbascums.

Suffolk

Helmingham Hall, near Ipswich.
See pages 161-3.

Lime Kiln, Claydon.
See pages 153-4.

Wyken Hall, Stanton.
The shrub rose garden is planted for exuberance within a formal framework. There are roses elsewhere in the gardens which are still being developed.

WALES

Clwyd.

Rhual, Mold.
Twenty-one box-edged beds in 18th century sunken parterre

garden of earlier house. Climbers and shrub roses elsewhere.

Dyfed

The Dingle, Crundale, Haverfordwest.
Peaceful, enclosed garden with all kinds of roses including weeping standards and climbers on arches and pergola.

Glamorgan

Dyffryn Gardens, St Nicholas, Cardiff.
Two large rose gardens, mostly modern roses.

The Clock House, Cathedral Close, Llandaff.
Collection of shrub and Species roses in small, walled garden.

Gwynedd

Bodnant, Tal-y-Cafn.
Two rose terraces one paved in stone, one in patterned brick, are just part of the famous gardens here. Good edging plants.

Maenan Hall, Llanwrst.
Roses throughout garden, particularly in walled garden.

SCOTLAND

For opening times of some properties see *Scotland's Gardens*, published by Scotland's Gardens Scheme.

Borders Region

Kailzie, Peebles.
A formal garden of Floribunda and H.T. roses behind a 20 ft stone wall.

Lochside, Yetholm, Kelso.
Fine collection of old roses and other rare plants in terraced garden.

Mellerstain, Gordon.
Formal gardens laid out in 1909 by Sir Reginald Blomfield include an intricate parterre planted with roses and a fine collection of shrub roses.

Monteviot, Jedburgh.
Terraced rose garden of old and modern roses.

Traquair House, Innerleithen.
Old roses on terrace of oldest inhabited house in Scotland.

Dumfries and Galloway Region

Brooklands, Crocketford.
Collection of old roses and other unusual plants in walled garden.

Fife Region

Hill of Tarvit, Cupar.
Small, concealed rose garden of house and gardens designed by Robert Lorimer in 1906.

Kellie Castle, Pittenweem.
One-acre Victorian walled garden with rose arches and shrub roses. Restored by National Trust for Scotland.

Grampian Region

Aberdeen.
The whole city is one big rose garden.

Tillypronie, Tarland.
Pretty, formal rose garden. Wonderful view.

Lothian Region

Malleny Garden, Balerno.
National Trust for Scotland.
Charming garden including the
NCCPG's collection of 19th
century roses.

Tyninghame, near East Linton.
Intimate, secret garden of old
roses.

Strathclyde Region

Biggar Park, Biggar.
Shrub rose garden.

Brodick Castle, Isle of Arran.
The walled kitchen garden was
developed as a rose garden by
Mary, Duchess of Montrose, and
has now been restored by the
National Trust for Scotland to its
original Victorian style.

Tayside Region

Edzell Castle, Angus.
Floribunda roses in early 17th
century parterre pattern.

House of Pitmuies, by Forfar.
Formal, enclosed rose garden with
lily pond and fountain, trelliswork
and rose bower. Also roses elsewhere in garden.

NORTHERN IRELAND

Ardress House, Co. Armagh.
National Trust.

Dixon Park, Belfast.

Mount Stewart, Co. Down.
National Trust.

Rowallane, Co. Down.
National Trust gardens include a
walled garden of old roses.

EIRE

Birr Castle, Co. Offaly.
Muckross Garden, Co. Kerry.
Powerscourt, Co. Wicklow.
St Anne's Rose Garden, Dublin.

AUSTRALIA

CANBERRA

Parliament House.

NEW SOUTH WALES

Auburn Botanic Garden, Sydney.
Civic Centre Garden, Wagga
Wagga.
Crematorium Rose Gardens,
Beresford.
Gore Hill Cemetery, Westbourne
Street, Gore Hill
Jesmond Park, Newcastle.
Lambton Park, Newcastle.
Pioneer Park, Wollongong.

Rockwood Cemetery, East Street,
Lidcombe.
Roxborough Park, Baulkham
Hills.
Royal Botanic Garden,
Sydney.

QUEENSLAND

Elizabeth Park Gardens, Marybor-
ough.
New Farm Park, Brisbane.

SOUTH AUSTRALIA

Ashford Hospital Garden,
Adelaide.
Botanic Garden, Adelaide.
David Ruston Garden, Renmark.
The Flower Garden, Watervale.
Veale Rose Garden, Adelaide.

TASMANIA

Botanic Gardens, Hobart.

Carr Villa Crematorium,
Launceston.
Glenorchy C.C. Admin. Offices,
Hobart.
Old University Reserve, Hobart.
Presentation Convent,
Launceston.
Roseneath Reserve, Hobart.
Royal Park, Launceston.
Sixways Corner, Launceston.
Tolosa Street Water Reserve,
Hobart.
West Park, Burnie.

VICTORIA

Alistair Clark Memorial Rose
Garden, St Kilda, near Melbourne.
Benalka Rose Garden, Melbourne.
Botanic Garden, Geelong.
Eastern Park, Geelong
'Heide', Templestowe Road,
Bulleen.
Melbourne University.

'Rippon Lea', Hotham Street, Elsternwick.

Royal Botanic Gardens, Budwood Avenue, South Yarra.

Springvale Crematorium, Melbourne.

Victoria State Rose Garden, Wirribee Park Estate, Melbourne.

WESTERN AUSTRALIA

Cambridge Rose Garden, Floreat Park.

Kings Park Road Garden, West Perth.

Old Farm, Strawberry Hill, Albany.

Peace Memorial Gardens, Medlands.

Ross Roses, St Andrews Terrace, Willunga.

Zephyr Brook Heritage Rose Garden, Penjana.

FRANCE

For opening times see Green Michelin guides or *Guide des 300 Plus Beaux Jardins de France* by Philippe Thebaud.

Alsace-Lorraine
Jardin Botanique de Metz, Rue de Pont-à-Mousson, Metz.

Parc de l'Orangerie, Avenue de l'Europe, Strasbourg.

Parc de la Pépinière, Place de Gaulle, Nancy.

Aquitaine
Jardins d'Arnaga, Cambo-les-Bains.

Auvergne-Limousin
Château de Chavaniac-la-Fayette.

Jardin Lecoq, 7 Avenue Vercingétorix, Clermont-Ferrand.

Parc de l'Allier, Vichy.

Roseraie Municipale, Limoges.

Bourgogne–Franche-Comté
Parc Saint-Nicholas, Châlon-sur-Saône.

Centre–Poitou–Charentes
Château de Touffou, Bonnes, Vienne.

Jardin des Prés Fichaux, Bd. de la République, Bourges.

Parc Floral de la Source, Orléans.

Champagne–Nord–Picardy
Jardin des Plantes, Lille.

Paris–Ile de France
Château de la Celle-les-Bordes.

Jardins de Bagatelle.

Jardins Kahn, 5 Quai de Quatre-Septembre, Hauts-de-Seine.

Parc de Malmaison.

Roseraie de L'Haÿ-les-Roses.

Tarn-et-Garonne
La Roseraie du Parc de Chambord, Montauban.

Normandy
Jardin des Plantes, Rouen.

NEW ZEALAND

NORTH ISLAND

Parnell Rose Garden, Auckland.

City Council Rose Garden, Gisborne.

Civic Rose Garden, Hamilton.

King Edward Park, Hawerea.

Frimley Park, Hastings.

Mitchell Park, Lower Hutt.

Churchill Memorial Park, Masterton.

Queen Elizabeth Park, Masterton.

Kennedy Park, Napier.

Kemp House, Keri Keri, Northland.

Pompallier House, Russell, Northland.

Waimate North Mission House, Waimate, Northland.

Dugald MacKenzie Rose Garden, Palmerston North.

Murray Winton Garden, Rotarua.

Stratford Hospital Garden, Stratford.

Belmont Rose Garden, Takapuna.

Bolton Street Cemetery, Wellington.

Lady Norwood Rose Garden, Wellington.

City Rose Garden, Whangarei.

SOUTH ISLAND

Centennial Rose Garden, Blenheim.

Christchurch Rose Garden, Christchurch.

Linwood Avenue Crematorium, Christchurch.

Mona Vale Rose Garden, Christchurch.

Botanic Gardens, Dunedin.

Green Island Memorial Garden, Dunedin.

Invercargill Rose Garden, Invercargill.

Broadgreen Rose Garden, Nelson.

Garden of Memories, Oamaru.

Trevor Griffiths Display Garden, Timaru.

Queenstown Rose Garden, Queenstown.

UNITED STATES OF AMERICA

* denotes All-American Rose Selections trial or display gardens.

ALABAMA

Arlington House, Birmingham.

Birmingham Botanical Gardens, Birmingham.

ARIZONA

Reid Park Rose Garden, Tucson.

CALIFORNIA

Berkeley Municipal Rose Garden.

*Descanso Gardens, La Canada.

*Exposition Park, Los Angeles.

Golden Gate Rose Garden, San Francisco.

Huntingdon Botanical Gardens, San Marino.

Inez Parker Memorial Rose Garden, Balboa Park, San Diego.

Morcom Amphitheater of Roses, Oakland.

Rose Hills Memorial Park, Whittier.

COLORADO

Denver Botanic Gardens.

CONNECTICUT

Bruce Park, Greenwich.

Elizabeth Park, Hartford.

Norwich Memorial Rose Garden, Mohegan Park, Norwich.

Pardee Rose Garden, East Rock Park, Hamden.

DISTRICT OF COLUMBIA

Bishops Garden, Washington DC.

Dumbarton Oaks, Washington DC.

Franciscan Monastery, Quincy' Street, Washington DC.

Hillwood, Linnean Avenue, Washington DC.

FLORIDA

*Cypress Gardens, Winter Haven.

Four Arts Garden, Palm Beach.

Leu Gardens, Orlando.

Mounts Horticultural Learning Center, West Palm Beach.

Ringing Museums, Sarasota.

GEORGIA

142 Bull Street, Savannah.

Massee Lane, Fort Valley.

State Botanical Garden, Athens.

*Thomasville Nurseries, Thomasville.

IDAHO

Julia David Park, Boise.

Memorial Bridge Rose Garden, Lewiston.

Rotary Rose Gardens, Ross Park, Pocatello.

ILLINOIS

Chicago Horticultural Society Botanic Garden, Glencoe.

*Glen Oak Botanical Garden, Peoria.

Grant Park Rose Garden, Chicago.

Lake of the Woods Botanic Garden, Mahomet.

Marquette Park Rose Garden, Chicago.

*Merrick Park Rose Garden, Evanston.

Morton Arboretum, Lisle.

INDIANA

Hillsdale Gardens, Indianapolis.

Lakeside Park, Fort Wayne.

IOWA

Greenwood Park, Des Moines.

Huston Park, Cedar Rapids.

Iowa State Rose Society Garden, State Center.

*Iowa State University Rose Garden, Ames.

KANSAS

*E. F. A. Reinisch Rose Gardens, Gage Park, Topeka.

Kansas City Municipal Rose Garden, Huron Park.

KENTUCKY

Lexington Cemetery.

LOUISIANA

*American Rose Center, Shreveport.

Hodges Gardens, Many.

Rip Van Winkle Gardens, Jefferson Island.

MAINE

*Deering Oaks Rose Garden, Portland.

MARYLAND

*Brookside Gardens, Wheaton.

Ladew Topiary Gardens, Monkton.

William Paca Garden, Annapolis.

MASSACHUSETTS

Arnold Arboretum, Jamaica Plain.

Berkshire Garden Center, Stockbridge.

Naumkeag, Stockbridge.

*Stanley Park, Westfield.

MICHIGAN

Dow Gardens, Midland.

Matthai Botanical Gardens, Ann Arbor.

*Michigan State University Horticulture Gardens, East Lansing.

MINNESOTA

Lake Harriet Park, Minneapolis.

MISSISSIPPI

Mynelle Gardens, Jackson.

MISSOURI

*Capaha Park, Cape Girardeau.

Glendal Rose Gardens, Independence.

Laura Conyers Smith Rose Garden, Kansas City.

*Missouri Botanical Garden, St Louis.

MONTANA

Sunset Park Memorial Rose Garden, Missoula.

NEVADA

Idelwild Park, Reno.

NEW HAMPSHIRE

*Fuller Gardens, North Hampton.

Moffatt-Ladd House, Portsmouth.

NEW JERSEY

Frelinghuysen Arboretum, Morristown.

Lamertus C. Bobbink Memorial Rose Garden, Thompson Park, Lincroft.

NEW YORK

Brooklyn Botanical Garden.

*Dr E. M. Mills Memorial Rose Garden, Syracuse.

Edward De T. Bechtel Memorial Rose Garden, New York Botanical Garden, Bronx.

Everett A. Piester Memorial Garden, Cornell Plantations, Ithaca.

Lyndhurst, Tarrytown.

*Maplewood Rose Garden, Monroe County Parks Arboretum, Rochester.

Old Westbury Gardens.

Queens Botanical Garden, Flushing.

Roosevelt Rose Garden, Hyde Park.

Sonnenberg Gardens, Canandaigua.

Vanderbilt Historic Site, Hyde Park.

NORTH CAROLINA

Biltmore Estate, Asheville.

Bicentennial Garden, Greensboro.

*Reynolds Gardens, Wake Forest University, Winston-Salem.

*Tanglewood Park, Clemmons.

OHIO

Adena, Chillicothe.

Garden Center of Greater Cleveland.

Inniswood Botanical Garden, Westerville.

Lakeview Park Rose Garden, Lorain.

*Park of Roses, Columbus.

Michael H. Hovath Garden of Legend and Romance, Wooster.

Stan Hywet Hall, Akron.

OKLAHOMA

Will Rogers Horticultural Park, Oklahoma City.

*Woodard Park, Tulsa.

OREGON

George E. Owen Municipal Rose Garden, Eugene.

*International Rose Test Garden, Washington Park, Portland.

PENNSYLVANIA

Friends Hospital, Philadelphia.

*Hershey Gardens, Hershey.

Longwood Gardens, Kennett Square.

*Malcolm W. Gross Memorial Rose Garden, Allentown.

Marion W. Revinus Rose Garden, Morris Arboretum, Philadelphia.

*Robert Pyle Memorial Rose Garden, West Grove.

Swiss Pines, Malvern.

Wyck, Philadelphia.

RHODE ISLAND

Blithewood, Bristol.

Newport Mansions, Newport.

Roger Williams Park, Providence.

SOUTH CAROLINA

*Edisto Memorial Gardens, Orangeburg.

Hampton Park, Charleston.

TENNESSEE

Cheekwood, Nashville.

TEXAS

Samuel Grand Municipal Rose Garden, Dallas.

*Tyler Rose Garden, Tyler.

UTAH

*Salt Lake City Municipal Rose Garden.

VIRGINIA

Norfolk Botanical Garden.

Mount Vernon.

*River Farm, Mount Vernon.

Woodlawn Plantation, Mount Vernon.

Virginia House, Richmond.

WASHINGTON

Point Defiance Park, Tacoma.

Rose Hill, Manito Park, Spokane.

Woodlawn Park, Seattle.

WISCONSIN

*Boerner Botanical Gardens, Whitnall Park, Hales Corner.

Jones Arboretum and Botanical Gardens, Readstown.

*Olbrich Gardens, Madison.

Paine Art Center, Oshkosh.

Bibliography

Beales, Peter, *Classic Roses*, Collins Harvill, London, 1985

Brown, Jane, *Gardens of a Golden Afternoon*, Allen Lane, London, 1982

Bunyard, E. A., *Old Garden Roses*, Country Life, London, 1936

Fish, Margery, *Cottage Garden Flowers*, Collingridge, London, 1961

   Gardening in the Shade, Collingridge, London, 1964

Fleming, Lawrence and Gore, Alan, *The English Garden*, Michael Joseph, London, 1979

Foster-Melliar, the Revd A., *The Book of the Rose*, Macmillan, London, 1894

Gerard, John, *Historie of Plants*, London, 1597, facsimile edn. Bracken Books, London, 1985

Gibson, Michael, *The Book of the Rose*, Macdonald, London, 1980

   The Rose Gardens of England, Collins, London, 1988

Gore, Frances, *The Book of Roses or The Rose Fancier's Manual*, Colburn, London, 1838; reprinted Earl Coleman, New York, 1978

Hadfield, Miles, *A History of British Gardening*, Hutchinson, London, 1960

Hamden, Mary, *Rose Gardening*, Thornton Butterworth, London, 1921

Harvey, John, *Mediaeval Gardens*, Batsford, London, 1981

Hibberd, Shirley, *The Rose Book*, Groombridge, London, 1864

Hobhouse, Penelope, *Colour in your Garden*, Collins, London, 1985

   A Book of Gardening, Pavilion, London, 1986

Hole, Dean S. R., *A Book About Roses*, Blackwood, London, 1874

Jefferson, Thomas, *Garden Book 1766–1824*, reprinted Philadelphia 1985

Jekyll, Gertrude, *Colour Schemes for the Flower Garden*, Country Life, London, 1908

Jekyll, Gertrude and Mawley, Edward, *Roses for English Gardens*, Newnes, London, 1902

Le Rougetel, Hazel, *A Heritage of Roses*, Unwin Hyman, London, 1988

McFarland, J. Horace, *The Rose in America*, Macmillan, New York, 1923

Miller, Everitt L. and Cohen, Jay S., *The American Garden Guidebook*, Evans, New York, 1987

Page, Russell, *The Education of a Gardener*, Collins, London, 1962

Redouté, P. J. and Thory, *Les Roses*, Paris 1817 to 1824; Books 1 and 2 (facsimile), Ariel Press, London, 1954 and 1956

Robinson, William, *The English Flower Garden*, John Murray, London, 1883

   The Wild Garden, 1870

Sitwell, Sir George, *An Essay on the Making of Gardens*, Duckworth, 1909

Thacker, Christopher, *The History of Gardens*, Croom Helm, London, 1979

Thébaud, Philippe, *Guide des 300 Plus Beaux Jardins de France*, Rivages, Marseille, 1987

Thomas, Graham Stuart, *The Old Shrub Roses*, Dent, London, 1955

   Shrub Roses of Today, Dent, London, 1962

   Climbing Roses Old and New, Dent, London, 1965

   Perennial Garden Plants, Dent, London, 1976

   The Art of Planting, The National Trust, London, 1984

   Gardens of the National Trust, The National Trust, London, 1979

Williams, Dorothy Hunt, *Historic Virginia Gardens*, Charlottesville, 1974

Acknowledgements

This book grew from a seed first sown on a walk, in the country, in France, and for that I would like to thank Ariel Whatmore. I would never have considered writing it had I not been introduced to old roses some years ago by John Scarman, and I would like to thank him for sharing his infectious enthusiasm.

I am grateful to the following people for their kind help with research for the book: Mr Graham Stuart Thomas, O B E, V M H (and for permission to quote from his books), Mr William H. Potts, jun., M. Jean-Claude Daufresne, Mr Nicholas Day, Mr J. L. Priestley, and Mrs Tamara Talbot-Rice.

Garden visiting is always a pleasure, even in bad weather, but the pleasure is increased when owners are generous with their time and hospitality. On my visits to rose gardens, I met with this generosity wherever I went, from so many people that it is not possible to mention them all by name. Their kindness is not less appreciated if they do not appear in the following list: Mr Guy and the Hon. Mrs Acloque, Lady Ashbrook, Mr and Mrs Robin Brackenbury, the late Mr Humphrey Brooke, Mr and Mrs Randle Brooks, Mr and Mrs Kenneth Carlisle, Lord Crawshaw, Mrs Mary Dawes, Lord and Lady FitzWalter, Major and Mrs Basil Heaton, Mr and Mrs David Hodges, Mrs Daphne Hoskins, Mr and Mrs John Hubbard, Lady Serena James, Mr and Mrs Robert Lea, Mr and Mrs Julian Nicholson. Mr Michael Polhill, Mrs Frances Pumphrey, Mr and Mrs Charles Quest-Ritson, Dr J. A. Smart, Lady Suffolk, Lord and Lady Tollemache, Mr and Mrs Peter Wake, Mrs M. A. Willis, and Mrs Margaret Wray.

I would also like to thank the gardeners, whose work I interrupted, for their patience in answering my questions.

Tania Midgley travelled long distances to take photographs for the book, often at short notice and in unfavourable conditions. I am very grateful to her for taking so much trouble, and to Dick Balfour for his many helpful suggestions.

Finally, I want to thank those friends and relations who welcomed me as a self-invited guest during my tour of rose gardens, including Mr and Mrs Julian Carlisle, Mr Julian and the Hon. Mrs Cotterell, Mr Digby Durrant, Mr and Mrs John Lascelles, Captain and Mrs Robert Phillimore, Mr and Mrs John Scarman, Mr and Mrs Brian Thomas, Mr and Mrs Geoff White and Mr and Mrs Jon Wood.

For the illustrations thanks are due to the following:

R. C. Balfour 104, 125c; Biofotos 45, 105a; Bridgeman Art Library i, 17, 23, 39, 61; British Library 43a and b; Ediface 57 (G. Darley), 65a (G. Darley); Fine Art Photographic Library 41; Garden Picture Library vi (Perdereau/Thomas), 32 (Perdereau Thomas), 36a and b (Perdereau/Thomas), 56b (Gary Rogers), 65b (D. Fell), 65c (J. Pavia), 73d (Perdereau/Thomas), 81 (C. Boursnall), 84 (G. Rogers), 93 (M. Majerus), 109b (Perdereau/Thomas), 141a and b (M. Heuff); Giraudon 13, 25, 26; Derek Gould 73b, 121a, 125a, 137b; Sonia Halliday 9, 16a and b, 22; Jerry Harpur ii, 109a, 133; Photos Lamontagne 67a, 97a; Andrew Lawson 56a, 97b, 120c, 121b; Georges Lévêque 33, 137a; Mansell Collection 7, 12, 20, 67, 143; S. & O. Matthews 2, 5, 72, 73a, 85a and b, 105b, 137c; Tania Midgeley 6, 72b, 145, 148, 152, 160, 164, 165, 169; The National Trust 77, 85c, 89, 101, 117, 129; National Image 69 (R. Fletcher), 73c (B. Gibbons), 113 (R. Fletcher), 120a and c (B. Gibbons), 121c (R. Fletcher), 125b (B. Gibbons); Osterreichisches Nationalbibliothek 19; Photos Horticultural 49.

Picture research: Philippa Lewis.

Index

200